GILDA BRANCATO is an attorney in the Office of the Legal Adviser, United States Department of State. She previously served as law clerk to Judge Leonard I. Garth of the United States Court of Appeals for the Third Circuit and practiced law in Boston with Bingham, Dana & Gould. She is a graduate of the State University of New York at Stony Brook and the New York University School of Law, where she was Research Editor of the Law Review.

ELLIOT E. POLEBAUM is a lawyer in Washington, D.C., with the firm of Cleary, Gottlieb, Steen & Hamilton. He served as law clerk to Judge James L. Oakes of the United States Court of Appeals for the Second Circuit and Justice William J. Brennan, Jr., of the United States Supreme Court. He practiced law in Boston with Goodwin, Procter & Hoar and is a graduate of Middlebury College, the John F. Kennedy School of Government of Harvard University and the New York University School of Law, where he was Managing Editor of the Law Review.

Also in this Series

AN AMERICAN
CIVIL LIBERTIES
UNION HANDBOOK

THE RIGHTS OF POLICE OFFICERS

GILDA BRANCATO
ELLIOT E. POLEBAUM

General Editor of this series
Norman Dorsen, *President, ACLU*

A DISCUS BOOK/PUBLISHED BY AVON BOOKS

THE RIGHTS OF POLICE OFFICERS is an original publication of Avon Books. This work has never before appeared in book form.

AVON BOOKS
A division of
The Hearst Corporation
959 Eighth Avenue
New York, New York 10019

Copyright © 1981 by the American Civil Liberties Union (ACLU), Inc.
Published by arrangement with
the American Civil Liberties Union
Library of Congress Catalog Card Number: 80-69945
ISBN: 0-380-78352-5

First Discus Printing, September, 1981

DISCUS TRADEMARK REG. U. S. PAT. OFF. AND IN OTHER COUNTRIES, MARCA REGISTRADA, HECHO EN U. S. A.

Printed in the U.S.A.

10 9 8 7 6 5 4 3 2 1

Acknowledgments

We wish to thank Deputy Commissioner Kenneth Conboy of the New York City Police Department and Robert O'Neil, President of the University of Wisconsin, for their thoughtful review of portions of the manuscript. We also thank David Klafter for his editorial suggestions and cite-and-substance examination, and Jeanne Pitkewicz and Debra Trovato for their skillful secretarial assistance. Any shortcomings are of course our own.

G.B.
E.E.P.

For L.I.G., J.L.O.,
and W.J.B., Jr.

Contents

Preface

This guide sets forth your rights under present law and offers suggestions on how you can protect your rights. It is one of a continuing series of handbooks published in cooperation with the American Civil Liberties Union.

The hope surrounding these publications is that Americans informed of their rights will be encouraged to exercise them. Through their exercise, rights are given life. If they are rarely used, they may be forgotten and violations may become routine.

This guide offers no assurances that your rights will be respected. The laws may change and, in some of the subjects covered in these pages, they change quite rapidly. An effort has been made to note those parts of the law where movement is taking place but it is not always possible to predict accurately when the law *will* change.

Even if the laws remain the same, interpretations of them by courts and administrative officials often vary. In a federal system such as ours, there is a built-in problem of the differences between state and federal law, not to speak of the confusion of the differences from state to state. In addition, there are wide variations in the ways in which particular courts and administrative officials will interpret the same law at any given moment.

If you encounter what you consider to be a specific abuse of your rights you should seek legal assistance. There are a number of agencies that may help you, among them ACLU affiliate offices, but bear in mind that the ACLU is a limited-purpose organization. In many communities, there are federally funded legal service offices which provide assistance to poor persons who cannot afford the costs of legal representation. In general, the rights that the ACLU

11

defends are freedom of inquiry and expression; due process of law; equal protection of the laws; and privacy. The authors in this series have discussed other rights in these books (even though they sometimes fall outside the ACLU's usual concern) in order to provide as much guidance as possible.

These books have been planned as guides for the people directly affected: therefore the question and answer format. In some of these areas there are more detailed works available for "experts." These guides seek to raise the largest issues and inform the non-specialist of the basic law on the subject. The authors of the books are themselves specialists who understand the need for information at "street level."

No attorney can be an expert in every part of the law. If you encounter a specific legal problem in an area discussed in one of these handbooks, show the book to your attorney. Of course, he will not be able to rely *exclusively* on the handbook to provide you with adequate representation. But if he hasn't had a great deal of experience in the specific area, the handbook can provide helpful suggestions on how to proceed.

Norman Dorsen, Chairperson
American Civil Liberties Union

The principal purpose of this handbook, and others in this series, is to inform individuals of their legal rights. The authors from time to time suggest what the law should be, but the authors' personal views are not necessarily those of the ACLU. For the ACLU's position on the issues discussed in this handbook, the reader should write to Librarian, ACLU, 22 East 40th Street, New York, N.Y. 10016.

Introduction

The sensitivity and centrality of the police function in contemporary America cannot be overstated. The Supreme Court recognized in *Foley* v. *Connelie* that police officers

> are charged with the prevention and detection of crime, the apprehension of suspected criminals, investigation of suspect conduct, execution of warrants and have powers of search, seizure and arrest without a formal warrant under limited circumstances. In the course of carrying out these responsibilities an officer is empowered by New York law to resort to lawful force, which may include the use of any weapon that he is required to carry while on duty. . . .

> A discussion of the police function is essentially a description of one of the basic functions of government, especially in a complex modern society where police presence is pervasive. The police function fulfills a most fundamental obligation of government to its constituency. Police officers in the ranks . . . are clothed with authority to exercise an almost infinite variety of discretionary powers. The execution of the broad powers vested in them affects members of the public significantly and often in the most sensitive areas of daily life. . . . The exercise of police authority calls for a very high degree of judgment and discretion, the abuse or misuse of which can have serious impact on individuals. . . .[1]

Foley indicated that police officers play an integral role in enforcing and protecting the rights of citizens. What is often overlooked is that police officers also have rights as public employees and as citizens. First and foremost, the U.S. Constitution and the constitutions of most states guarantee freedom of speech, association, religion, and assembly, and guarantee due process and equal protection under law. Additionally, many federal and state statutes that are more protective than constitutional minimums apply to police officers. For example, Title VII of the 1964 Civil Rights Act protects state and local employees, including police officers, against discrimination based on race, color, national origin, gender, and religion.

Both police officers and applicants for police jobs have rights, although the rights may differ. For example, Chapter I discusses the qualifications a department often requires of applicants and employees, and the rules usually apply equally to both groups. By contrast, the due-process rights discussed in Chapter VI often extend greater protection to employees than to applicants. Generally speaking, the basic substantive rights which protect the two groups are similar, but important differences exist in the way these rights are enforced.

A person who is denied a job or fired for an apparently improper reason should try to ascertain the reason for the action. The applicant or the officer should remember that the reason given may not be the real reason. There may be established grievance procedures to help employees (and perhaps applicants) to learn the reason for discharge, demotion, or transfer (or refusal to hire). When a grievance procedure has been exhausted, the employee or applicant may seek outside assistance. Very often help must be sought first from a state agency, and then from a federal agency charged with enforcing the right asserted. Time limits within which an administrative complaint can be made are often strict, so that an officer should act quickly. After exhausting the proper administrative procedures, a person may seek a remedy in court.

If it is established that the department violated the law, the most obvious remedy for a wrongful denial of employment or discharge is an order that the department hire or rehire the wronged person. Courts may also order the payment of money damages to compensate for lost wages and perhaps for injury to professional reputation and employment opportunities. In extreme cases, where the department's bad faith has been established, additional damages may be awarded. The most common remedy sought, however, is to be hired or put back on the job, and this is the relief most commonly ordered.[2]

This handbook seeks to highlight the most essential rights that protect the law-enforcement officer. Every officer's job varies, of course, depending upon the size of the department, the size and character of the community, and the police officer's function, among other factors. So bear in mind that the general guidelines discussed here can vary depending upon your particular job. And bear in mind that this book paints with a broad brush: it provides a general guide to an officer's rights but cannot, practically speaking, discuss details and nuances or be relied on to provide specific legal advice. Needless to say, this is not a technical and operational handbook, nor a primer on criminal procedure. For this, you should check departmental regulations, guidelines, and handbooks, and consult the department's legal staff. This book focuses instead on the obligations of the government toward its law-enforcement officers. And as officers begin to appreciate their rights, their sensitivity to the rights of others should be enhanced.

Gilda Brancato
Elliot E. Polebaum
January 18, 1981

NOTES

1. 435 U.S. 291, 293, 297–98 (1978).
2. *See* R. O'NEIL, THE RIGHTS OF GOVERNMENT EMPLOYEES 21–22 (1978).

I

Qualifications for Employment

Does a person have a right to be a police officer?
Until relatively recently, no. In 1892, Justice Oliver
Wendell Holmes wrote that "a person may have a constitutional right to talk politics, but he has no constitutional
right to be a policeman." [1] Today the courts no longer
make such categorical statements. Instead, when examining
a police officer's claim for employment, courts balance it
against the reasons underlying the government's refusal
to take the action requested by the officer. This balancing
approach attempts to accommodate the legitimate but conflicting interests of the individual officer and the government.

As one would expect, balancing has produced mixed
results. For example, an officer who is refused a promotion based upon race has an extremely strong claim, in
light of the law's abhorrence of racial discrimination. [2] By
contrast, an applicant who is refused a police job because
of a criminal record will find the courts less sympathetic.
Rather, the court might rule that the government has a
strong interest in ensuring that those charged with law
enforcement are themselves law-abiding. [3] In short, in
determining whether a person has a right to become (or
remain) a police officer, it is important to scrutinize closely
both the strength of the person's claim and any legitimate
explanations that underlie the government's position.

This chapter explores the validity of miscellaneous qualifications, such as required age, height, and weight, absence
of criminal record, and veteran's status. Chapter II discusses the permissibility of using race, sex, and parenthood

as factors in hiring. Chapter III explores whether and when the decision to hire can be based on political belief and association, and Chapter V examines sexual preference and personal associations as elements in the hiring decision. While reading these chapters, bear in mind that a factor that cannot justify a refusal to hire likewise cannot usually justify a firing, demotion, or transfer.

May an applicant be refused a job as a police officer because of race, national origin, or color?

No. Under the Constitution and under Title VII of the 1964 Civil Rights Act, state and local employees, including police officers, may not be refused a job on the basis of race, national origin, or color.[4] There are no ifs, ands, or buts to this prohibition.

More problematic is the legality of job requirements which appear neutral on their face, but which have the effect of excluding large numbers of a racial or ethnic group. For example, a 5'8" height requirement for the police position may serve to exclude a disproportionately large number of Spanish-surnamed male officers, who, as the courts have noted, are generally smaller than other men. Testing requirements are treated in detail later (in Chapter II, on "Race and Sex Discrimination"), but a few generalizations can be ventured at this point. First, the Supreme Court has ruled that the U.S. Constitution protects against racial discrimination only if it is intentional—and not if it results merely from neutral requirements that have a disproportionately adverse impact on minority groups.[5] By contrast, courts have ruled that some federal civil-rights statutes protect against practices that have a numerically disproportionate impact on minorities.[6] Since these civil-rights statutes enacted by Congress have expressed a policy prohibiting all forms of discrimination, both purposeful and unintended, courts applying these statutes have afforded greater protection to a complainant.

May a police applicant be refused a job because of her sex?

No, except in very limited instances.

In general, federal statutes protect against employment discrimination based upon gender,[7] unless sex—that is, malehood—"is a bona fide occupational qualification reasonably necessary to the normal operation of [a] particular business or enterprise." [8] The Supreme Court has interpreted the "bona fide occupational qualification" (BFOQ) to be "an extremely narrow exception." [9] Thus, women can be excluded from a job only where strong factual evidence demonstrates that no woman can perform the job adequately.[10] Put another way, the exclusion of women is permissible only where the *"essence"* of job performance is undermined by the presence of women.[11]

Other questions concerning the hiring and firing of women and mothers are treated in Chapter II.

May United States citizenship be required for police officers?

Yes. The Supreme Court squarely considered the question in *Foley* v. *Connelie*,[12] and in sweeping language, upheld the constitutionality of a New York statute requiring that a state trooper be a U.S. citizen:

> the exercise of police authority calls for a very high degree of judgment and discretion, the abuse or misuse of which can have serious impact on individuals. The office of a policeman is in no sense one of "the common occupations of the community." . . . A policeman vested with the plenary discretionary powers we have described is not to be equated with a private person engaged in routine public employment or other "common occupations of the community" who exercises no broad power over people generally. Indeed, the rationale for the qualified immunity historically granted to the police rests on the difficult and delicate judgments these officers must often make.
>
> In short, it would be as anomalous to conclude that citizens may be subjected to the broad discretionary powers of noncitizen police officers as it would be to say that judicial officers and jurors with power to judge citizens can be aliens. It is not surprising, therefore, that most States expressly confine the employment of police officers to citizens, whom the State may reasonably presume to be more familiar with and sympathetic to American traditions. Police

officers very clearly fall within the category of "important nonelective . . . officers who participate directly in the . . . *execution* . . . of broad public policy." . . . In the enforcement and execution of the laws the police function is one where citizenship bears a rational relationship to the special demands of the particular position. A State may, therefore, consonant with the Constitution, confine the performance of this important public responsibility to citizens of the United States.[13]

In 1978, when *Foley* was decided, thirty-six states required that state law-enforcement officers be citizens (Alabama, Arizona, Arkansas, California, Florida, Georgia, Hawaii, Idaho, Illinois, Indiana, Iowa, Kansas, Kentucky, Maine, Massachusetts, Michigan, Mississippi, Missouri, Montana, Nevada, New Hampshire, New Jersey, New Mexico, New York, North Dakota, Ohio, Oklahoma, Oregon, Pennsylvania, Rhode Island, South Dakota, Tennessee, Texas, Utah, Vermont, and West Virginia).[14] In light of the Supreme Court's explicit approval of this qualification for law-enforcement officers, other states may follow suit.

Some states, such as Oklahoma, also require that state law-enforcement officers be citizens of the state.[15]

Can a municipal police officer be required to live within the city limits?

Usually, but not always. The Supreme Court has upheld the constitutional validity of municipal-residency requirements,[16] but at least one state court has ruled that a municipality that enacted such a requirement lacked the power to impose the rule.[17] Thus, a municipal-residency requirement is valid where the local authorities have expressly or impliedly been accorded the power by the state to enact it.

Municipal practice varies widely. A city might require only that at the time of appointment to the police force, a person be a resident of the city or of a neighboring county. But many cities make residence within city limits a condition of employment.[18] Such requirements have been challenged on the ground that they abridge the constitutional right of public employees to travel freely. In a short opinion in March 1976, however, the Supreme Court held that a Philadelphia firefighter named McCarthy could be dismissed because he had moved out of the city.[19] Accordingly, appropriately defined and uniformly enforced bona fide residency requirements appear to be valid under the U.S. Constitution.[20]

Several courts have identified the special interests that residency laws may serve. One federal court of appeals sustained the rule requiring Cincinnati public school teachers to live within the city,[21] holding that the rule may serve several valid governmental objectives with respect to the city work force: a commitment to an urban school system, a closer involvement in the welfare of the city government, greater contact and familiarity with urban problems, and a higher degree of racial integration in the work force itself (since the proportion of minority-group members is often higher in the central city than in the adjacent suburbs).[22] While such a rule sharply restricts the choices of public employees and applicants, municipal interests have prevailed under federal constitutional law.

State law may differ, however. In a unanimous decision issued in April 1980, New York's highest court overturned New York City's residency rule for its uniformed forces, including police officers. The Court of Appeals reasoned that only the states—not cities—could regulate the right of civil servants to live where they wished:

> While the structure and control of the municipal service departments . . . may be considered of local concern within the meaning of municipal home rule, the residence of their members, unrelated to job performance or departmental organization, is a matter of state-wide concern not subject to municipal home rule.[23]

The court also ruled that the city requirement was inconsistent with state legislation: the state Public Officers Law prohibits a residency restriction for police officers in departments of over two hundred officers.

Charles Peterson, president of the Patrolmen's Benevolent Association (the New York City police union), welcomed the decision. Mayor Edward Koch, who pushed for residency legislation during his election campaign, stated that he would seek state legislation that allows cities to pass residency rules. Proponents of the measure contend that it will benefit the city's economy and promote civic concern. But the city's prior residency rule was repealed in 1962 in an attempt to attract better workers.[24]

May a department require residency for a certain period of time before a person may apply to become a police officer?

Yes, but only for a short period.

The Supreme Court has not ruled directly on this question. It did uphold a requirement of *actual* residency in the *McCarthy* case,[25] and has also approved a requirement of residency for the short period of time needed to ascertain actual bona fide residency. Still, on three occasions, the Court invalidated longer waiting requirements of, for example, one year, for the government benefits of public assistance, voting, and emergency medical care.[26] Longer waiting periods are generally invalid because they distinguish between two classes of actual residents solely on the basis of time of arrival. Although the courts might treat police employment differently from the public benefits noted above because of the police officer's special connection to the government,[27] a waiting period for police employment that is longer than three months would probably be held invalid.

May a city give preference in employment to longer-term residents?

The answer is unclear. If a waiting period imposed on new residents is invalid, so too may be a preference granted to longer-term residents. On the other hand, a preference may be more acceptable than the absolute prohibition imposed by a waiting period. For example, the Massachusetts Supreme Judicial Court has held that a town could give priority in its employment policies to people who had lived there for a year or more.[28] Since newcomers were not completely barred, and the preference could therefore be overcome in particular cases, the court upheld the preference.

May a police officer be forced to retire at a certain age? *
Under the Constitution, yes.

Mandatory retirement ages exist for a fair number of public jobs. [The legality of such requirements under the Age Discrimination in Employment Act will be discussed later.] In most instances, retirement becomes compulsory at sixty, sixty-five, or even at seventy—ages that correlate with a decline in strength, agility, and other qualities needed in a public worker. Several times, the Supreme Court has summarily affirmed decisions of lower courts upholding requirement ages.[29] A somewhat different case was presented, however, by Officer Robert Murgia, who was forced to retire from the Massachusetts state police force at age fifty. Since he was in perfect health and anxious to continue working, Murgia brought suit challenging the constitutionality of the law. A federal district court struck down the age-fifty retirement rule, finding it arbitrary in relation to the valid state interest in having healthy and alert police officers.[30] Not only was Murgia himself in perfect health, but there was evidence that other officers in their late forties were actually healthier than colleagues in their early forties.

The Supreme Court disagreed with the lower court and found that the Massachusetts rule rationally served the state's interest in a healthy state police force.[31] Although there may be exceptions, medical evidence showed that people do become more susceptible to heart attacks and other disabilities with increasing age. Identifying the exceptions (among whom Murgia might well be one) would be costly and time-consuming. Since the relationship between the rule and the governmental interest need only be "rational" and not a perfect fit, the existence of better alternatives was not critical. In the course of this decision —significant far beyond the narrow legal issue—the Court redefined the constitutional status of public employment: "This Court's decisions give no support to the proposition

* This and the following two questions and answers are adapted from Robert O'Neil's *The Rights of Government Employees* (New York: Avon Books, 1978). New material is enclosed in brackets; minor changes, such as changes in verb tense, capitalization, and footnote numbering, are not noted.

that a right of government employment per se is fundamental." [32] The meaning of this statement requires brief explanation. Where certain "fundamental" interests are involved—for example, the right to travel from state to state, or to vote—any restrictions are to be tested by a standard of "strict scrutiny." In all other contexts, a merely "rational basis" will suffice. There was little doubt that the age-fifty retirement rule would not have passed "strict scrutiny" had the interest in public employment been deemed "fundamental." But since the individual interest was not a "fundamental" one, a much looser nexus between the interest [government employment] and the classification [officers over fifty] was acceptable.

[Under the federal Age Discrimination in Employment Act, however, early mandatory retirement is probably invalid. This statute is discussed in detail later in this chapter.]

May a government agency refuse to hire people over a certain age? *

As a matter of constitutional law, there is no clear precedent. [Again, as we shall discuss later, statutes may disallow age restrictions.]

In the *Murgia* case, the Court had no occasion to consider another part of the Massachusetts law, which limited initial eligibility for the state police to persons between the ages of twenty-five and thirty. Government occupations that have early retirement rules typically also have age limits for hiring. There has been no separate constitutional test of such limits. Under the *Murgia* decision, however, it would seem that if the retirement part of the law is constitutionally valid, the same reasoning would apply to sustain the limits on starting age. If a police officer is too old to be reliable at age fifty, then presumably a state may decide that only persons under thirty can be trusted for rookie training—or that the state's investment in a police officer is so large that service of less than twenty years will not bear adequate return. Whatever the reason, the *Murgia* case almost certainly validates such . . . limits.[33]

---

* See footnote to previous question.

May a person be denied employment because he or she is too young? *

Many government occupations require that a person attain a certain age to be eligible. In states where the age of majority has been lowered to eighteen, a substantial group of new adults may be denied access to public employment. In one case that has considered this issue, the Supreme Court of New Jersey held that the age-twenty-one requirement of a city police force had been superseded by the lowering of the age of majority.[34] This decision simply interpreted New Jersey laws, and might or might not be followed in other states. The Constitution does not require that all aspects of adulthood go together, though the New Jersey decision is persuasive in terms of the legislature's probable intent in making eighteen-year-olds generally eligible for civic rights and responsibilities.

Does federal statute provide protection against hiring or firing based upon age?

Yes. The rules we have just discussed and the Supreme Court's decision in *Murgia* consider only *constitutional* protections. As we observed earlier, statutes often provide broader protection than the Constitution. In 1967, Congress enacted the Age Discrimination in Employment Act (ADEA).[35] The law forbids discrimination based on age against employees who are between forty and seventy.[36] Under the ADEA, workers are protected from being rejected for employment, transferred, denied a promotion, or fired because of age, unless the employer can demonstrate a clearly legitimate reason for its conduct.

Does the ADEA prohibit the automatic retirement of a police officer?

Probably.

Like Title VII of the 1964 Civil Rights Act, the ADEA contains a BFOQ exception.[37] Accordingly, age limitations for employment are valid when they can be justified as bona fide safety measures.[38] Put another way, age restrictions for the police might be a BFOQ if the government demonstrated that such restrictions were closely related in fact to the purposes which they sought to achieve. Conversely,

* See footnote to preceding questions.

age requirements founded upon mere stereotypes and un-tested assumptions are not permissible.

In *Houghton* v. *McDonnell-Douglas Corp.*,[39] a fifty-two-year-old chief production test pilot was transferred and ultimately fired because of his age. He alleged that his transfer violated the ADEA. The Eighth Circuit Court of Appeals agreed, ruling that the airplane manufacturer failed to demonstrate "a factual basis for believing that *substantially all* of the older pilots are unable to perform the duties of test pilot safely and efficiently *or* that *some* older pilots possess traits precluding safe and efficient job performance *unascertainable other than through* knowledge of the pilot's *age*." [40] Thus, the manufacturer failed to prove a BFOQ. Accordingly, if the test pilot was still physically able to perform his duties safely and efficiently, he was entitled to reinstatement and back pay. Three circuit courts, however, have upheld the Federal Aviation Administration (FAA) in its strict refusal to grant exemptions to its age-sixty rule, which prohibits pilots from operating airplanes after reaching age sixty.[41] With pilots eight years older than Houghton, and with a strong administrative responsibility to ensure safety, the appeals court said that a strict cutoff was reasonable. Unless medical predictions become reliable enough to permit individual determinations and exemptions from the age-sixty rule, the FAA is not abusing its discretion by refusing exemptions across the board.

Courts faced with the question whether police officers could be fired because of age would probably apply the analysis used in *Houghton*, invalidating the regulation unless compelling safety requirements and inadequate medical information, as in the FAA cases, justified an age limit.[42] If the government showed a factual basis for believing that older police officers were unable to perform their job safely and efficiently, the court would inquire whether any criteria other than age could be used by police departments to ascertain whether older officers performed safely and efficiently. Such other criteria include acuity of sight and hearing, agility, speed, good physical health, and the like. Unless the government demonstrated that substantially all officers of a certain age could not perform effectively, or that there existed no criteria other than age for weeding out ineffective officers, a court would probably rule that an older police officer who can do the job cannot be compelled to retire or transfer.

Further protection against age discrimination is provided by a recent amendment to the ADEA, which expressly disallows use of a seniority system or employee benefit plan that requires or permits the across-the-board retirement of employees under the age of seventy.[43] It is unclear, however, whether this new provision protects employees under all existing retirement plans, since courts have differed on whether the amendment should be applied retroactively.[44] Furthermore, the ADEA disallows the compulsory retirement before age sixty-five of an employee who is working in an executive or high policy-making position and who is entitled to a pension of at least $27,000 per year. A police chief or administrator who is covered by this provision could not be forced to retire until age sixty-five.[45]

Of course, a police officer or administrator who can no longer perform the job safely or effectively can be compelled to retire. Indeed, if employers have been tolerating less than competent performance from older workers who were approaching a set retirement age now prohibited by the ADEA, those employers may be forced to resort to firing the employee for cause, instead of trying to enforce the retirement age.[46]

Does the ADEA prohibit an age limit for first becoming a police officer?

Maybe. The ADEA protects persons between ages forty and seventy. Once an employee within the protected age class, or the administrative agency, makes out an initial complaint, the employer must justify the age limit as a BFOQ.[47] In a case brought by Philadelphia security officers, the city offered no technical analysis or statistics for cutting off applications at age forty-one, and a federal district court invalidated the requirement.[48] But in another case, a bus company produced evidence that it would be unsafe generally to consider new applicants over forty and that it would be impractical and unreliable to evaluate each applicant's ability to perform adequately. Therefore, the district court accepted a BFOQ defense, which the appeals court affirmed.[49]

In short, the ADEA gives police applicants between forty and seventy a legal basis for a suit that will force the police departments to justify their age limits, but the ADEA does not prevent the departments from presenting adequate factual evidence to support their regulations.

What are the procedures for bringing claims under the ADEA?

A person must bring a charge of age discrimination before the Equal Employment Opportunity Commission within 180 days after the alleged act of age discrimination (or within 300 days of the act if the person had already filed a claim with a state authority having the power to grant or seek relief from age discrimination).[50] The 180-day period may be extended if the person is not properly advised of the requirement by the federal department or is misled by the employer about the permanency of the the firing or transfer.[51] The charge of discrimination should consist of a written statement that identifies the potential defendant and describes in general terms the act that is believed to be discriminatory.

An individual who has filed a charge with the federal agency must wait sixty days before instituting an age-discrimination lawsuit in court.[52] The court action must be brought within two years after the act that is claimed to be discriminatory, or within three years if the act is alleged to be a willful violation of the ADEA.[53] These "limitations" periods are "tolled" (that is, they do not run) for up to one year while the federal agency attempts conciliation efforts between the employee and the charged defendants.[54]

If there is a state agency that handles age-discrimination complaints, an employee must file a charge with the state agency before filing a charge with the federal agency.[55] In such instances, the state agency must be allowed sixty days to act on the complaint before the federal agency can act.[56] Many states have an antidiscrimination statute and agency, so police officers should consult with local authorities first.

An officer who charges an ADEA violation and seeks money damages may have a jury trial on "any issue of fact." [57] An officer who proves the case can recover particularized economic damages such as lost wages, lost fringe benefits, and other lost earnings. The majority of courts have held, however, that an age-discrimination victim cannot recover damages for pain and suffering, mental anguish, damages to professional reputation, and similar kinds of consequential damages.[58] As for punitive damages—damages that do not compensate the victim for loss but punish the offender and thereby deter future wrongdoers—courts have held that they may not be recovered in an ADEA action.[59] But punitive damages are effectively available in another form, because if the employer's violation is willful (that is, knowing and intentional), a plaintiff will be entitled to "liquidated damages," in an amount equal to lost wages and benefits.[60] Because liquidated damages are awarded *in addition to* compensatory damages, one district court has said that liquidated damages effectively double the recovery for back pay and benefits.[61]

In addition, the ADEA expressly provides that plaintiffs may recover reasonable attorneys' fees if they prevail in the case.[62] But the statute does not provide attorneys' fees for employers, so that defendants who prevail can recover only if they meet the standard for judicially imposed fees by proving that the plaintiffs brought the court action in bad faith.[63]

Can a minimum height or weight be required?

Probably not. In *Dothard* v. *Rawlinson*, the Supreme Court ruled that height and weight standards that exclude disproportionately large numbers of women are invalid unless the employer demonstrates that they bear a direct relationship to job performance.[64] The *Dothard* Court invalidated an Alabama law requiring that state prison guards be at least 5′2″ and weigh at least 120 pounds, since the law excluded disproportionate numbers of women and was not essential to the demands of the job. This decision seems to end the use of arbitrary height-weight eligibility standards, and thus opens many jobs in law-enforcement agencies to women and to small men.[65]

Before *Dothard*, many courts and agencies had modified height and weight minimums that adversely affected women and small men. For example, the federal district court in Washington, D.C., struck down a 5′7″ height requirement as not rationally related to being a firefighter.[66]

Similarly, the U.S. Civil Service Commission has ruled invalid both the height and weight rules for the National Park Police, in the absence of any scientific proof of the relationship between such criteria and the demands of the job.[67]

The question now becomes whether height and weight standards can in fact be reasonably linked to job performance. The Supreme Court initially agreed to review the job-relatedness of a 5'7" height requirement for firefighters, but ultimately did not decide the issue.[68] That height requirement excluded 41 percent of the Mexican-Americans who applied to be firefighters. The government alleged that the requirement was related to the ability to handle firefighting equipment and was therefore justified, but the Ninth Circuit disagreed and invalidated the restriction. Although the Supreme Court vacated the Ninth Circuit's decision on procedural grounds, the court of appeals' opinion provides still another example of a physical requirement struck down for lack of job-relatedness. Moreover, again faced with a height requirement, the Ninth Circuit in *Blake* v. *City of Los Angeles* reversed a district court decision upholding the 5'6" minimum standard of the Los Angeles police force.[69] Judge Hufstedler explained that the rule, which excluded a disproportionate number of women applicants from the force, did not significantly correlate with the minimum strength purportedly required to subdue suspects; thus the rule was not justified by business necessity. The Court also invalidated physical-ability tests used by the Los Angeles police as exclusionary and unjustified.

May a police officer be fired or not hired if highly overweight?

Probably, if substantial excess weight is shown to be disabling to the proper performance of a police officer's duties. Indeed, one convict escaped from the custody of a 215-pound police officer who was unable to give chase.[70]

May a police officer be required to meet requirements of physical health, speed and agility, mental health, and educational achievement?

Yes, once it has been demonstrated that the physical or mental health requirement is reasonable and job-related.[71] Courts differ, however, as to the proof required to show job-relatedness. Some courts require a factual showing that a physical or mental requirement is justified by business necessity.[72] Other courts apply a less demanding standard; one, for example, upheld a strong-back requirement for manual laborers as *presumptively* job-related.[73] In the "strong-back" case, the court dispensed with the need for actual proof that the requirement was job-related, even though it potentially had a racially discriminatory effect. The First Circuit Court of Appeals has held that a swimming test is permissible (in the absence of racially disproportionate impact) and that requiring a high-school education or an honorable military discharge reflects a valid "compelling interest" of the states.[74] By comparison, in *Blake* v. *City of Los Angeles*, the Ninth Circuit invalidated physical-ability tests which were not justified by business necessity. Although the cases appear inconsistent, one matter is undisputed: irrational or arbitrary job requirements are never permissible, as a matter of constitutional law.

May a police officer be denied or dismissed from employment because of a criminal record or act?

Probably. The answer ultimately depends upon the nature, seriousness, and timing of the criminal offense.

An isolated and minor offense might not justify a refusal to hire or a dismissal, as long as no evidence suggested that the officer's job performance was affected.[75] But, if it is shown that employing a former offender would undermine efficiency or discipline, or the morale of other officers, a firing or refusal to hire would probably be valid.[76] Without question, it is permissible where the police applicant has committed a felony.[77] Indeed, courts have consistently upheld such exclusions, embracing the rationale that a former felon might be thought to lack the qualities of discipline, honesty, and self-control that the police position demands and the public has come to expect.[78]

Departmental guidelines similar to those adopted in New York City provide some protection against the automatic exclusion of former misdemeanants. New York City's guidelines read as follows:

The following are among the factors which would ordinarily be cause of disqualification [from employment]: (a) conviction for an offense, the nature of which indicates lack of good moral character or disposition toward violence or disorder; (b) repeated conviction for an offense, where such convictions indicate a disrespect for the law; (c) repeated discharge from employment, where such discharge indicates poor performance or inability to adjust to discipline; (d) addiction to narcotics or excessive use of alcoholic beverages. In accordance with provisions of law, persons convicted of a felony or receiving a dishonorable discharge from the Armed Forces are not eligible for appointment to this position. Persons convicted of petit larceny may be declared ineligible for appointment.

May a police officer be refused employment because of participation in a methadone-maintenance or other drug-rehabilitation program?

Yes. In 1979 the Supreme Court ruled on a New York Transit Authority policy terminating or denying employment for those who used methadone sometime during the past five years.[79] A group of job applicants, including one who had formerly been a highly competent transit employee, brought suit, challenging the validity of the methadone bar.[80] The district court and court of appeals invalidated the policy on constitutional grounds.[81] The Supreme Court reversed, and in a 6-3 decision, ruled that the policy furthered the objectives of safety and efficiency and conformed to constitutional and statutory mandates.[82] In the face of a lower-court finding that the bar had a racially discriminatory effect, the Supreme Court ruled that the job-relatedness of the policy rebutted any presumption of racial discrimination.[83] The Court also ruled that the policy was rational, not unprincipled, and concerned "matters of personnel policy that do not implicate [constitutional] principle." [84] Three Justices dissented, observing that the policy was racially discriminatory, or irrational and unjustified.[85]

Here, specific legislation might be enacted to provide a measure of protection which the Constitution does not afford. One federal law provides that "No person may be denied or deprived of Federal civilian employment or a Federal profession or other license or right solely on the ground of prior drug abuse," [86] but the law does not apply to the FBI, CIA, or other positions designated as "sensitive," and, of course, to state and local police forces.

May written examinations be required of police applicants?

That depends. Written examinations that gauge verbal skills and reading comprehension have some relevance to job performance. Written tests become suspect, however, when they result in the exclusion of a disproportionate number of minority-group applicants. At this point it becomes necessary to ascertain whether the exam is "in fact directly related to the requirements" of the police program.[87] If not, it will violate Title VII and possibly other civil-rights statutes that prohibit discrimination based on race, color, national origin, or sex.[88]

May a police applicant or employee be compelled to disclose financial data?

Yes. Police officers can be refused a job or fired for failure to furnish financial information upon request.

The point was decided in *O'Brien* v. *DiGrazia*.[89] Patrol officers in Boston's police force were ordered to complete a financial questionnaire listing all sources of income for the officer and spouse, all their "significant assets," and estimates of expenditures over the past five years, and to enclose copies of federal and state tax returns. Officers who refused were given a hearing, then suspended without pay for thirty days. The First Circuit Court of Appeals found no grounds for relief. Having no reason to believe that the financial data would be broadcast to the public or other government agencies, the court of appeals found that the officers' privacy interests were not invaded, particularly in light of "society's [strong] interest in an honest police force." [90] Moreover, the court ruled that the disclosure order, which was specific, narrow, and directly related to official duties, did not infringe the officers' right against self-incrimination; nor did it deter their exercise of First Amendment guarantees.[91] In short, the court found the order directly and reasonably related to the job requisites of honesty and lack of corruption. As such, the court did not require the Boston Police Commissioner to demonstrate even a reasonable basis for suspicion of the questioned officers.[92]

May veterans be given preference in hiring?

Yes. The United States Supreme Court has held that veteran-preference statutes are constitutionally permissible in nearly every shape and form.[93] They may be subject to challenge under antidiscrimination statutes, however.

At issue in *Personnel Administrator of Massachusetts v. Feeney* [94] was the Massachusetts statute giving veterans an absolute preference over nonveterans for public employment.[95] Unlike other state statutes and the federal civil-service statute, which grant extra points to veterans in evaluating their application, the Massachusetts scheme mandated that any veteran be appointed over a nonveteran, even if substantially less qualified. Helen Feeney charged that the statute had a severely discriminatory impact on women, since only 2 percent of Massachusetts veterans are women.[96] Moreover, less drastic measures, such as a point system, were available to compensate veterans for military service. Nonetheless, the Supreme Court upheld the constitutionality of the statute. Justice Stewart ruled that the statute was not enacted with the purpose of discriminating against women but rather reasonably effectuated the permissible goal of assisting both male and female veterans to find employment.

Veteran-preference statutes that adversely affect women may still be challenged under Title VII, since in *Feeney* the Court considered only the constitutional validity of the statute. Moreover, redress may be sought through state legislation. This avenue may be particularly useful for constituents who seek replacement of an unusually harsh preference system with a point system that attempts to harmonize the goals of equalizing employment opportunities for women and assisting veterans in the job market.[97]

NOTES

1. McAuliffe v. Mayor & Board of Aldermen, 155 Mass. 216, 29 N.E. 517 (1892).
2. *E.g.*, Brown v. Board of Educ., 349 U.S. 294 (1954); Title VII of the Civil Rights Act of 1964, 42 U.S.C.

§2000e *et seq.* (1976) [hereinafter Title VII]; 42 U.S.C. §§1981, 1983 (1976).

3. See cases cited note 78 *infra.*
4. U.S. Const. amend. XIV; Title VII; 42 U.S.C. §§1981, 1983 (1976).
5. Village of Arlington Heights v. Metropolitan Hous. Dev. Corp., 429 U.S. 252, 264–71 (1977); Washington v. Davis, 426 U.S. 229, 239–45 (1976). *But see* Castaneda v. Partida, 430 U.S. 482, 492–501 (1977) (discriminatory intent inferred from stark pattern of underrepresentation of minorities on grand juries).
6. *See, e.g.,* Dothard v. Rawlinson, 433 U.S. 321 (1977) (sex discrimination in prison employment); United States v. City of Chicago, 573 F.2d 416 (7th Cir. 1978) (discriminatory promotions by the fire department); Metropolitan Hous. Dev. Corp. v. Village of Arlington Heights, 558 F.2d 1283 (7th Cir. 1977). *cert. denied,* 434 U.S. 1025 (1978) (housing discrimination); Kinsey v. First Regional Sec., Inc., 557 F.2d 830, 839–40 (D.C. Cir. 1977) (employment discrimination); United States v. City of Chicago, 549 F.2d 415 (7th Cir.), *cert. denied,* 434 U.S. 875 (1977) (police department employment discrimination). *But cf.* Guardians Ass'n v. Civil Serv. Comm'n, 49 U.S.L.W. 2154, 23 Fair Empl. Prac. Cas. 677 (2d Cir. July 25, 1980) (discrimination count under §1981).
7. Title VII; Equal Pay Act of 1963, 29 U.S.C. §206 (1976); 42 U.S.C. §1983 (1976).
8. Title VII §703(e), 42 U.S.C. §2000e–2(e) (1976).
9. Dothard v. Rawlinson, 433 U.S. 321, 334 (1977).
10. *See* Weeks v. Southern Bell Tel. & Tel. Co., 408 F.2d 228, 235 (5th Cir. 1969).
11. Diaz v. Pan Am. World Airways, 442 F.2d 385, 388 (5th Cir.), *cert. denied,* 404 U.S. 950 (1971) (emphasis in original).
12. 435 U.S. 291 (1978).
13. *Id.* at 299–300 (emphasis in original) (footnotes and citations omitted).
14. *See id.* at 299 n. 8. *See also* Chavez-Salido v. Cabell, 49 U.S.L.W. 2006 (C.D. Cal. June 4, 1980) (requirement that "peace officer" be citizen is unconstitutionally overbroad, although statute narrowly drawn to cover police officer alone would be valid).
15. 435 U.S. at 299 n. 8.

16. McCarthy v. Philadelphia Civil Serv. Comm'r, 424 U.S. 645 (1976) (per curiam).
17. *See* N.Y. Times, Apr. 30, 1980, at B1, Col. 5–6.
18. R. O'NEIL, THE RIGHTS OF GOVERNMENT EMPLOYEES 29 (1978).
19. McCarthy v. Philadelphia Civil Serv. Comm'r, 424 U.S. 645 (1976) (per curiam). *Accord,* Detroit Police Officers Association v. City of Detroit, 385 Mich. 519, 190 N.W. 2d 97 (1971), *appeal dismissed,* 405 U.S. 950 (1972).
20. Shapiro v. Thompson, 394 U.S. 618 (1969).
21. Wardwell v. Board of Educ., 529 F.2d 625 (6th Cir. 1976). *See also* Mogle v. Sevier County School Dist., 540 F.2d 478 (10th Cir. 1976), *cert. denied,* 429 U.S. 1121 (1977); Pittsburgh Fed'n of Teachers v. Aaron, 417 F. Supp. 94 (W.D. Pa. 1976).
22. O'NEIL, *supra* note 18, at 30.
23. *See* N.Y. Times, Apr. 30, 1980 at B1, Col. 5–6.
24. *Id.*
25. 424 U.S. 645 (1976).
26. Memorial Hosp. v. Maricopa County, 415 U.S. 250 (1974) (emergency hospital services); Dunn v. Blumstein, 405 U.S. 330 (1972) (voting); Shapiro v. Thompson, 394 U.S. 618 (1969) (public assistance).
27. *See* Foley v. Connelie, 435 U.S. 291 (1978).
28. Town of Milton v. Civil Serv. Comm'n, 365 Mass. 368, 312 N.E.2d 188 (1974); *see* Holland v. Bligh Const. Co., 61 Ill.2d 258, 335 N.E.2d 469 (1975).
29. Weisbrod v. Lynn, 383 F. Supp. 933 (D.D.C. 1974), *aff'd,* 420 U.S. 940 (1975). McIlvaine v. Pennsylvania, 454 Pa. 129, 309 A.2d 801 (1973), *appeal dismissed,* 415 U.S. 986 (1974).
30. Murgia v. Massachusetts Bd. of Retirement, 376 F. Supp. 753 (D. Mass. 1974) *rev'd,* 427 U.S. 307 (1976).
31. Massachusetts Bd. of Retirement v. Murgia, 427 U.S. 307 (1976). [*Accord,* Vance v. Bradley, 440 U.S. 93 (1979)] (upholding mandatory retirement age of 60 for participants in foreign service because requirement rationally furthered Congress's objective that foreign service participants be professionally competent and physically reliable); Malmed v. Thornburgh, 48 U.S.L.W. 2767 (3d Cir. May 13, 1980) (upholding mandatory retirement age of 70 for state judges), *petition for cert. filed,* 49 U.S.L.W. 3176 (U.S. Sept. 5, 1980) (No. 80–361).
32. 427 U.S. at 313.

33. *Cf.* Usery v. Tamiami Trail Tours, Inc., 531 F.2d 224 (5th Cir. 1976). *Compare id. with* Rodriguez v. Taylor, 428 F. Supp. 1118 (E.D. Pa. 1976), *vacated in part,* 569 F.2d 1231 (3d Cir. 1977), *cert. denied,* 436 U.S. 913 (1978).

34. New Jersey State Police Benevolent Ass'n v. Town of Morristown, 65 N.J. 160, 320 A.2d 465 (1974).

35. Pub. L. No. 90–202, 81 Stat. 602 (1967) (codified as amended at 29 U.S.C. §§621 *et seq.* (1976)).

36. *See* Pub. L. No. 95–256, 92 Stat. 189 (1978) (codified at 29 U.S.C.A. §631(a) (West Supp. 1979)).

37. 29 U.S.C. §623(f) (1976).

38. *See* Dothard v. Rawlinson, 433 U.S. 321, 334 (1977).

39. 553 F.2d 561 (8th Cir.), *cert. denied,* 434 U.S. 966 (1977).

40. *Id.* at 564 (emphasis supplied). *Accord,* 46 U.S.L.W. 57 (May 9, 1978) (analyzing the 1978 amendments to ADEA).

41. 14 C.F.R. §121.383(c) (1979). The cases are Rombough v. Federal Aviation Adm'n, 594 F.2d 893 (2d Cir. 1979); Gray v. Federal Aviation Adm'n, 594 F.2d 793 (10th Cir. 1979); Starr v. Federal Aviation Adm'n, 589 F.2d 307 (7th Cir. 1979).

42. *See* cases cited notes 39 & 41 *supra.*

43. Pub. L. No. 95–256, 92 Stat. 189 (1978) (codified at 29 U.S.C.A. §623(f)(2) (West Supp. 1979)) (effective Apr. 4, 1978), *superseding* United Air Lines v. McMann, 434 U.S. 192 (1977), which had held that retirement pursuant to a bona fide plan was not an impermissible strategy for avoiding the ADEA.

44. *See* Jensen v. Gulf Oil Refining Co., 49 U.S.L.W. 2174, 23 Fair Empl. Prac. Cas. 790 (5th Cir. Aug. 8, 1980); Smart v. Porter Paint Co., 49 U.S.L.W. 2174, 23 Fair Empl. Prac. Cas. 764 (7th Cir. Aug. 7, 1980). *Compare* Marshall v. Eastern Airlines, 474 F. Supp. 364 (S.D. Fla. 1979), *and* Davis v. Boy Scouts of America, 457 F. Supp. 665 (D.N.J. 1978), *with* Marshall v. Delaware River & Bay Auth., 471 F. Supp. 886 (D. Del. 1978); Marshall v. Atlantic Container Line, 470 F. Supp. 71 (S.D.N.Y. 1978), *and* Marshall v. Baltimore & Ohio R.R., 461 F. Supp. 362 (D. Md. 1978).

45. Pub. L. No. 95-256, 92 Stat. 189 (1978) (codified at 29 U.S.C.A. §631(c)) (West Supp. 1979) (effective January 1, 1979).

46. 46 U.S.L.W. 57 (May 19, 1978) (analyzing the 1978 amendments to ADEA).

47. Usery v. Tamiami Tours, Inc., 531 F.2d 224 (5th Cir. 1976) (no applications for initial employment between 40 and 65); Rodriguez v. Taylor, 428 F. Supp. 1118 (E.D. Pa. 1976), *vacated in part*, 569 F2d 1231 (3d Cir. 1977), *cert. denied*, 436 U.S. 913 (1978) (no applications for Philadelphia security officer over 41).

48. *Id.*

49. Usery v. Tamiami Tours, Inc., 531 F.2d 224 (5th Cir. 1976).

50. 29 U.S.C. §§626(d), 633(b) (1976 & Supp. 1979); Dartt v. Shell Oil Co., 539 F.2d 1256 (10th Cir. 1976), *aff'd by an equally divided Court*, 429 U.S. 1089 (1977) (per curiam). *Cf.* Mohasco Corp. v. Silver, 444 U.S. 990 (1979) (granting petition for certiorari). *Compare* Ciccone v. Textron, Inc., 49 U.S.L.W. 2635 (1st Cir. Mar. 17, 1980), *with* Bean v. Crocker Nat'l Bank, 600 F.2d 754 (9th Cir. 1979).

51. H.R. Rep. No. 95–950, 95th Cong., 2d Sess. 12 (1978). Coke v. General Adjustment Bureau, 48 U.S.L.W. 2781 (5th Cir. May 7, 1980) (employer misrepresentation). *See* Wright v. Tennessee, 49 U.S.L.W. 2137 (6th Cir. Aug. 11, 1980) (en banc).

52. 29 U.S.C.A. §626(d) (West Supp. 1978).

53. *Id* §§255, 626(e) (1976).

54. *Id.* §626(e)(2) (West Supp. 1978).

55. *Id.* §633(b) (1976); Oscar Mayer & Co. v. Evans, 441 U.S. 750 (1979); Reich v. Dow Badiche Co., 575 F.2d 363 (2d Cir. 1978), *cert. denied*, 439 U.S. 1009 (1979); Curry v. Continental Airlines, 513 F.2d 691, 693 (9th Cir. 1975); Fitzgerald v. New England Tel. & Tel. Co., 459 F. Supp. 996 (D. Mass. 1978).

56. 29 U.S.C. §633(b) (1976).

57. 29 U.S.C.A. §626(c) (West Supp. 1978). *Accord,* Lorillard v. Pons, 434 U.S. 575 (1978). *See* Hidalgo v. Nakshian, 49 U.S.L.W. 3401 (U.S. Dec. 1, 1980) (granting petition for certiorari), *reviewing* 48 U.S.L.W. 2572 (D.C. Cir. 1980) (employee suing government under ADEA §15(c) has right to trial by jury).

58. 29 U.S.C. §626(c) (1976); Walker v. Pettit Constr. Co., 605 F.2d 128, 129–30 (4th Cir. 1979); Slatin v. Stanford Research Inst., 590 F.2d 1292, 1295 & n. 3 (4th Cir. 1979); Vazquez v. Eastern Airlines, 579 F.2d 107 (1st

Cir. 1978); Dean v. American Security Ins. Co., 559 F.2d 1036 (5th Cir. 1977), *cert. denied,* 434 U.S. 1066 (1978); Rogers v. Exxon Researching & Eng'r. Co., 550 F.2d 834 (3d Cir. 1977), *cert. denied,* 434 U.S. 1022 (1978) (no recovery permitted for pain and suffering), *overruled on other grounds,* Holliday v. Ketchum, Mac-Leod & Grove, Inc., 584 F.2d 1221 (3d Cir. 1978) (en banc); Douglas v. American Cyanamid Co., 472 F. Supp. 298 (D. Conn. 1979); Riddle v. Getty Ref. & Marketing Co., 460 F. Supp. 678 (N.D. Okla. 1978) (damages for emotional distress and mental anguish not recoverable under ADEA); Schlicke v. Allen-Bradley Co., 448 F. Supp. 252 (E.D. Wis. 1978). *But see* Bertran v. Orkin Extermination Co., 432 F. Supp. 952 (N.D. Ill. 1977) (pain and suffering held recoverable).

59. *E.g.,* Dean v. American Security Ins. Co., 559 F.2d 1036 (5th Cir. 1977); Riddle v. Getty Ref. & Marketing Co., 460 F. Supp. 678 (N.D. Okla. 1978). *See* 46 U.S.L.W. 55 (May 9, 1978) (analysis of 1978 amendments to ADEA).

60. 29 U.S.C. §626(b) (1976). *See* Rodriguez v. Taylor, 428 F. Supp. 1118 (E.D. Pa. 1976), *affirmed in relevant part,* 569 F.2d 1231 (3d Cir. 1977), *cert. denied,* 436 U.S. 913 (1978).

61. Buchholz v. Symons Mfg. Co., 445 F. Supp. 706 (E.D. Wis. 1978).

62. 29 U.S.C. §626(b) (1976), *incorporating* 29 U.S.C. §216(b) (1976); Rodriguez v. Taylor, 428 F. Supp. 1118 (E.D. Pa. 1976), *vacated in part on other grounds,* 569 F.2d 1231 (3d Cir. 1977), *cert. denied,* 436 U.S. 913 (1978).

63. Cova v. Coca-Cola Bottling Co., 574 F.2d 958, 962 (8th Cir. 1978).

64. 433 U.S. 321 (1977). *Accord,* Vanguard Justice Soc'y, Inc. v. Hughes, 471 F. Supp. 670, 716–17 (D. Md. 1979). *See generally* Comment, *Height Standards in Police Employment,* 47 S. CAL. L. REV. 585 (1974).

65. While the Court in *Dothard* struck down arbitrary physical requirements, it found adequate justification as a BFOQ for excluding women from "contact positions" at maximum-security all-male prisons. *See* Chapter II, text accompanying notes 46–49, 55.

66. *See* Fox v. Washington, 396 F. Supp. 504 (D.D.C. 1975).

67. *See* O'NEIL, *supra,* note 18, at 36.

68. County of Los Angeles v. Davis, 99 S. Ct. 1379 (1979), *vacating and remanding on grounds of mootness,* 566 F.2d 1334 (9th Cir. 1978).

69. 595 F.2d 1367 (9th Cir. 1979), *cert. denied,* 100 S. Ct. 1865 (1980).

70. New York Times, June 4, 1975, at 59, col. 4.

71. Harless v. Duck, 22 Fair Empl. Prac. Cas. 1073 (6th Cir. 1980), *cert. denied,* 49 U.S.L.W. 3249 (U.S. Oct. 6, 1980) (No. 80–86) (invalidated physical ability test having disparate impact on women applicants and not job-related); Hardy v. Stumpf, 21 Cal. 3d 1, 145 Cal. Rptr. 176, 576 P.2d 1342 (1978) (upheld requirement that police applicants scale six foot wall). *See* Washington v. Davis, 426 U.S. 229 (1976). *Cf.* Kelley v. Johnson, 425 U.S. 238 (1976); Smith v. United States Air Force, 566 F.2d 957 (5th Cir.), *cert. denied,* 439 U.S. 819 (1978).

72. Blake v. City of Los Angeles, *supra* note 69. *See also* Cleveland Bd. of Educ. v. LaFleur, 414 U.S. 632 (1974) (individualized determination principle); Gurmankin v. Constanzo, 556 F.2d 184 (3d Cir. 1977) (same).

73. Hardy v. Stumpf, 21 Cal. 3d 1, 145 Cal. Rptr. 176, 576 P.2d 1342 (1978); Smith v. Olin Chemical Corp., 555 F.2d 1283 (5th Cir. 1977) (en banc).

74. Castro v. Beecher, 459 F.2d 725 (1st Cir. 1972). *See* Jackson v. Curators of Univ. of Mo., 456 F. Supp. 879 (E.D. Mo. 1978) (two-year college requirement for campus patrol officers upheld as business necessity).

75. *See* Young v. Hampton, 568 F.2d 1253 (7th Cir. 1977); Osterman v. Paulk, 387 F. Supp. 669 (S.D. Fla. 1974).

76. *Cf.* Kelley v. Johnson, 425 U.S. 238 (1976). *See also* Neaveill v. Andolsek, 577 F.2d 749 (7th Cir.) (aff'g mem. unreported district court opinion), *summarized* at 47 U.S.L.W. 3253 (No. 78–315), *cert. denied,* 439 U.S. 965 (1978).

77. *See* Lewis v. United States, 48 U.S.L.W. 4205 (U.S. Feb. 27, 1980) (upholding statute prohibiting former felon from possessing firearm, even if conviction allegedly erroneous); Richardson v. Ramirez, 418 U.S. 24 (1974) (upholding disenfranchisement of convicted felons); De-Veau v. Braisted, 363 U.S. 144 (1960) (upholding statute barring former felons from holding office in waterfront labor union); Giles v. United States, 553 F.2d 647 (Ct. Cl. 1977) (valid dismissal of tax investigator who filed

late returns); Taffel v. Hampton, 463 F.2d 251 (5th Cir. 1972) (evidence showed connection between dismissal and efficient government service); McGarvey v. District of Colum., 468 F. Supp. 687 (D.D.C. 1979) (upholding exclusion of former felons from all public employment).

78. Upshaw v. McNamara, 435 F.2d 1118 (1st Cir. 1970); McGarvey v. District of Colum., 468 F. Supp. 687 (D.D.C. 1979); Hetherington v. California State Personnel Bd., 82 Cal. App. 3d 582, 147 Cal. Rptr. 300 (1978); McCain v. Sheridan, 160 Cal. App. 2d 174 (1958). Cf. Toro v. Malcolm, 44 N.Y.2d 146, 404 N.Y.S. 2d 558, cert. denied, 439 U.S. 837 (1978) (upholding application to corrections officer of New York statute vacating public office upon incumbent's felony conviction; upon voluntary reinstatement after reversal of conviction on appeal, no entitlement to back pay).

79. New York City Transit Authority v. Beazer, 440 U.S. 568 (1979).

80. 399 F. Supp. 1032, 1052 (S.D.N.Y. 1975).

81. 558 F.2d 97 (2d Cir. 1977), aff'g 399 F. Supp. 1032 (S.D.N.Y. 1975).

82. 440 U.S. at 587–92.

83. Id. at 587.

84. Id. at 592.

85. Id. at 597 (Brennan, White, Marshall, JJ., dissenting).

86. 21 U.S.C. §1180(c) (1976).

87. Washington v. Davis, 426 U.S. 229, 251 (1976).

88. United States v. City of Chicago, 549 F.2d 415 (7th Cir.), cert. denied, 434 U.S. 875 (1977); Firefighters Inst. v. City of St. Louis, 549 F.2d 506 (8th Cir.), cert. denied, 434 U.S. 819 (1977). See Washington v. Davis, 426 U.S. 229 (1976); Kinsey v. First Regional, Inc., 557 F.2d 830 (D.C. Cir. 1977) (dictum); Pennsylvania v. Operating Eng'r, Local 542, 47 U.S.L.W. 2486 (E.D. Pa. Jan. 2, 1979); Allen v. City of Mobile, 464 F. Supp. 433 (S.D. Ala. 1978).

89. 544 F.2d 543 (1st Cir. 1976), cert. denied, 431 U.S. 914 (1977). Cf. Plante v. Gonzalez, 575 F.2d 1119 (5th Cir. 1978), cert. denied, 439 U.S. 1129 (1979) (state senators may be compelled to disclose financial data).

90. 544 F.2d at 546.

91. Id.

92. Id. at 546 n. 4.

93. Personnel Adm'r of Mass. v. Feeney, 99 S. Ct. 2282

(1979). *Accord,* Ballou v. Department of Civil Serv., 75 N.J. 365, 382 A.2d 1118 (1978).
94. 99 S. Ct. 2282 (1979).
95. Mass. Gen. Laws. Ann. ch. 31, §26 (West).
96. 99 S. Ct. at 2291.
97. *E.g.,* Massachusetts House Bill No. 1742 (1980). *See* Feeney, 99 S. Ct. at 2290 n. 16.

II

Race and Sex Discrimination

RACE DISCRIMINATION

Like all employees, law-enforcement officers are protected under Title VII of the 1964 Civil Rights Act [1] (and possibly other civil-rights statutes such as Section 1983 [2]) against exclusionary employment practices based on race. Categorically, decisions to hire, promote, and fire cannot be based on discrimination against minorities. The body of discrimination law that protects police officers is essentially identical to the law pertaining to all other public employees. Accordingly, the reader should consult the treatment of race discrimination in employment in *The Rights of Racial Minorities*, by E. Richard Larson and Laughlin McDonald (New York: Avon Books, 1980; pp. 63-94), and the excellent (although slightly older) treatment of race (and sex) discrimination in Robert O'Neil's *The Rights of Government Employees* (New York: Avon Books, 1978; pp. 125-39). These two ACLU handbooks discuss both the substance of an employee's rights and the procedures to follow to protect those rights. This chapter treats only those aspects of race discrimination law which most commonly affect police officers.

Are written examinations for appointment as a police officer valid?

Yes, unless the examination results exclude a disproportionately large number of minority recruits and are not directly job-related.[3] In such instances they may not be used.

The use of police entry exams varies among municipalities. New York City, for example, stopped using written police tests in 1973, but adopted a controversial written examination in 1979 which has generated court battles.[4] Most police departments use medical, psychological, or character tests. Such tests, incidentally, often result in a high rate of failure for all applicants. To avoid heavy costs in future medical disability payments, New York City recently tightened its medical standards to screen out back, heart, and hearing problems.[5] Since then, New York's failure rate rose from a historical 50 percent to 62 percent. The administration of medical tests is generally valid, however, unless test results disproportionately exclude female or minority-group members and are not job-related.[6]

How does a court analyze the validity of a written examination?

Under the Constitution's equal-protection clause, the applicants must show that the examination intentionally discriminated against minorities.[7] This is difficult to establish. If discriminatory purpose is not proven, the plaintiffs lose; if it is proven, the plaintiffs will undoubtedly win, since the government will have an almost impossible task trying to justify its discriminatory conduct.[8]

Under Title VII, the standards are more favorable to applicants. A court's Title VII analysis of a written examination follows three steps:

1. The complaining party must first make out a prima facie case of discrimination, i.e., show that the test selects applicants in a racial pattern significantly different from that of the pool of applicants.
2. If an employer then meets its burden of proving that its tests are "job-related,"
3. the complaining party must show that other tests, without undesirable racial effect, would also serve the employer's interest in "efficient and trustworthy workmanship."[9]

If the government fails to establish Step 2 after the applicants prove Step 1, the test is invalid.

What test results are "prima facie" discriminatory?

There is no set formula for weeding out exclusionary exams. The 1978 guidelines of the federal Equal Employment Opportunity Commission (EEOC) include as discriminatory any testing and selection procedures which have an *adverse impact* on the employment opportunities of a race, sex, or ethnic group.[10] The EEOC guidelines were jointly adopted by the EEOC, the Civil Service Commission, the Justice Department, and the Labor Department.[11] Agencies which have not adopted the guidelines (including most police departments) and courts probably would require a substantial adverse impact in order to find a prima facie case of discrimination. Such a showing was made recently by blacks and Hispanics challenging New York City's written exam.[12] The exam was prepared by the City Department of Personnel, which tried to ensure that it was "not culturally biased." [13] Administered in June 1979 the test consisted of one hundred multiple-choice questions. The city claims that it required only an eighth-grade reading level and no knowledge of police procedures. Applicants taking the exam were given written explanations of laws or circumstances under which arrests could be made, and were then asked to answer questions based on the given explanations. Four sample questions follow:

1. Nancy Sanders sees a diamond ring on the sidewalk of a busy street. She picks it up, and decides to keep it. According to the definitions given, Sanders
    (a) committed the crime of burglary
    (b) committed the crime of larceny
    (c) committed the crime of robbery
    (d) did not commit any of the crimes defined in the alphabetical listing
2. Ted Whitney likes to annoy people on crowded subway trains by making obscene gestures at them. According to the definitions given, when Ted Whitney makes such gestures he commits the crime of
    (a) harassment
    (b) jostling
    (c) menacing
    (d) sexual misconduct
3. Sid Jime, in order to obtain sexual gratification,

touches the sexual parts of women, without their consent, on crowded subway trains. According to the definitions given, Jime committed the crime of
- (a) criminal mischief
- (b) rape
- (c) sexual abuse
- (d) sexual misconduct

4. Bill Lear, intending to scare John Baker, drives his vehicle toward Baker at high speed. Baker quickly jumps out of the vehicle's path and, as Lear turns his vehicle toward Baker, Lear narrowly misses Craig Charles, a bystander. Neither Charles nor Baker is injured. According to the definitions given, Lear
- (a) did not commit a crime
- (b) did not commit an assault against Baker or Charles
- (c) committed an assault against Charles only
- (d) committed an assault against Baker and Charles [14]

Blacks and Hispanics constituted 31 percent of the 36,797 applicants who took the exam, but only 15.4 percent of those who passed.[15] The Guardians Association, a group representing the City's black police officers, and the Police Hispanic Society brought suit, challenging the exam as biased and unrelated to police work.[16] The federal district court invalidated the department's use of the test, finding that a written exam alone cannot assess an applicant's ability to perform police work. The city filed an appeal with the Second Circuit Court of Appeals.

Under what circumstances are written examinations job-related?

There is no clear answer. The Supreme Court initially agreed to review the validity of a written test for fire-fighters but ultimately determined not to decide the case on the merits.[17] Courts, then, continue to rule on the content validity of exams on a case-by-case basis.

The 1978 EEOC guidelines, for example, permit the use of an examination having exclusionary impact only if justified by a legitimate business necessity [18]—a difficult standard which the employer must prove. Moreover, the guidelines prescribe that employers administering an exam conduct a "validity study," which would include an investigation of suitable alternative selection procedures and alternative methods of using the same selection procedure that have as little adverse impact as possible. Also, the EEOC guidelines require an employer to justify a cutoff or a rank-order method that is used to score an exam.[19]

Police departments would at least be required to demonstrate a relationship between performance on the written examination and requirements of the police job or training program.[20] Moreover, many courts require that entry examinations be justified by business necessity and meet other EEOC standards.[21] Establishing business necessity therefore becomes the critical issue. Sergeant Frank Miranda, the president of the Police Hispanic Society, has observed "The best test of a cop comes during his probation and how he actually stands up in the stress of the job, not by some pencil-and-paper test." Commissioner McGuire has countered that the New York City written test was "fair" and "job related," and was administered only after a strong minority recruitment drive and special tutoring for the exam.[22]

What remedies may be granted to victims of discriminatory practices?

There are usually five remedies a court may impose on a department that is found to have discriminated:

1. An order to hire, reinstate, or promote the employee or employees against whom discrimination has been practiced.[23]
2. An injunction against the repetition or continuation of the practice found to be discriminatory.
3. An award of back pay or actual wages that the victims of discrimination would have earned had the discrimination not been practiced.
4. An order adopting an affirmative-action program for minority hiring in the department.[24]
5. In extraordinary cases, an award of punitive damages against a department found to have discriminated in bad faith.[25]

In the case of discriminatory written examinations, the courts have also imposed orders blocking the appointment

of new police recruits who were hired in part based on
the defective examinations. The district court employed
this remedy in the New York City examination suit, pro-
voking outcries about resulting personnel shortages. The
problem was remedied when the city agreed to abide by
the court's minority-hiring plan, and 500 new recruits
came on board.[26]

Can a court order race-conscious affirmative-action programs as a remedy for proven past discrimination?

Yes.[27]

In *United Steelworkers of America* v. *Weber*, the U.S.
Supreme Court considered whether Title VII of the 1964
Civil Rights Act permits a private employer to adopt a
race-conscious affirmative-action program that set aside
50 percent of the openings in an on-the-job training
program for minority workers.[28] The employer had voluntarily adopted the program on the basis of well-known
historical racial imbalances in the industry, but without
an official finding of past discrimination. The *Weber* Court
upheld the validity of the strict numerical hiring plan. In
the situation where past discrimination by a department
is officially *proven*, the case for approving a numerical
plan is even stronger.

Since police departments are government authorities,
their conduct must conform to constitutional requirements
as well as to Title VII. In *Regents of the University of
California* v. *Bakke*, the Supreme Court upheld the constitutionality of considering race as a factor in public
programs.[29] In *Bakke*, the Court reviewed the validity of
a strict affirmative-action program adopted by the medical
school at the University of California at Davis. The university did not have a proven record of racial discrimination,
but rather sought to mitigate the long-standing underrepresentation of minority candidates in the medical profession. The Court invalidated the strict numerical
program but approved the consideration by public agencies
of "race as a factor" in admissions, and hiring.

Without question, court remedies that seek to undo prior
discriminatory practices of police departments can consider the race of applicants. More problematic is defining
the extent to which race can be considered. Judicially
imposed remedies of numerical hiring plans are probably

valid under *Bakke*,[30] since numerical hiring goals may be the only effective measure to undo past, proven discrimination.[31] EEOC Chairperson Eleanor Holmes Norton, for one, has interpreted *Bakke* to permit virtually all governmental and court-imposed affirmative action that responds to past discrimination—including goals and timetables.[32] The courts agree. In *Association against Discrimination in Employment* v. *City of Bridgeport*, a case decided after *Bakke*, the court ordered the Bridgeport fire department to adhere to a hiring formula designed to remedy the discriminatory impact of written qualification examinations.[33] Under the formula, the fire department was ordered to accept all otherwise qualified minority candidates who had not passed the exam. The department was also ordered to comply thereafter with a quota hiring system, until it employed a total of 125 black and Hispanic firefighters. Similarly, in the lawsuit invalidating New York City's written examination as discriminatory, the district court ordered that 50 percent of New York City's police recruits be black or Hispanic. The Second Circuit Court of Appeals reduced to one-third the figure for minority-hiring, pending its full review of the district court order.

May a police department voluntarily adopt affirmative-action programs in the absence of an official finding of past discrimination?

This is an open question

Although the *Weber* Court validated affirmative-action programs voluntarily adopted by private employers, the Supreme Court has not ruled whether government employers may voluntarily adopt strict numerical plans in the absence of an official finding of past discrimination.[34] The adoption of voluntary plans is important, however, because minority representation on police forces has historically been low.[35]

In 1979, in *Detroit Police Officers Association* v. *Young,* the Sixth Circuit Court of Appeals held that the Detroit police department could voluntarily adopt an affirmative-action plan for the promotion of black officers.[36] The court ruled that a preferential hiring plan that seeks to alleviate an imbalance caused by traditional practices of job segregation is reasonable and permissible. The court elaborated that use of a voluntary affirmative plan is proper where (1) it was adopted to correct substantial and chronic minority-group underrepresentation, (2) the plan reasonably utilizes race without stigmatizing any group or individual, and (3) the numerical program is the sole means of achieving the plan's goals.[37] EEOC guidelines adopted in 1978 also approve voluntary affirmative-action programs—independent of any court-imposed remedy—as vehicles to accomplish the purposes of Title VII.[38] The Supreme Court will at some point have to decide the validity of such programs.

Where a police force is racially imbalanced, a department can certainly adopt voluntary affirmative hiring policies that are less strict than a numerical quota. Affirmative-action requirements that mandate goals (but not quotas) set general ranges of hiring in which minority candidates may be given special consideration.

SEX DISCRIMINATION

Which laws protect police officers against sex discrimination in employment?

The basic source of protection for women, as for minorities, is Title VII of the Civil Rights Act of 1964,[39] which was extended in 1972 to cover all public employment, including police departments.[40] Title VII forbids discrimination based on sex, except where sex is a "bona fide occupational qualification" (BFOQ) for the position.[41]

Also important is the Equal Pay Act of 1963, which guarantees equal compensation for equal work.[42] Equal work is defined as work that requires the same skill, effort, and responsibility.[43] Most state and local government positions and many federal positions are covered by the Equal Pay Act, except for elective and policy-making positions.

Section 1983 of the post-Civil War civil rights laws applies to sex discrimination as well as to discrimination based on race.[44] That law gives a right of redress to any person whose civil rights are denied by any other person acting "under color of state law." "State color" includes all state and local, but not federal, employment. Finally, many states and municipalities have enacted their own fair-employment laws prohibiting discrimination on grounds of sex as well as race. The Massachusetts Equal Pay Act, for example, requires that equal pay be given for "work of like or comparable character" [45]—a more flexible standard than equal pay for equal work. State and local laws and their applicability to public employment vary.

When is sex (malehood) a "bona fide occupational qualification" (BFOQ) for employment?

In *Dothard* v. *Rawlinson,* the Supreme Court held the BFOQ to be an extremely limited exception.[46] Here the Court found such a limited exception in the position of "contact" guard in the potentially dangerous setting of an all-male, maximum-security prison. The *Dothard* Court based its holding on undisputed evidence that the mere presence of women posed a substantial security problem in the prison. A BFOQ may be found, then, where strong factual evidence demonstrates that no woman can perform the job safely or adequately.[47]

The EEOC has issued guidelines defining the BFOQ.[48] The guidelines declare that only business necessity, and not merely business convenience, will justify gender-based distinctions. Such distinctions must be judged not on the basis of "stereotyped characterizations of the sexes" or "characteristics generally attributed to the group" but rather on the basis of "individual capacities" of the particular employee. Further, sex as a BFOQ must be justified in terms of the peculiar requirements of the particular job. Under these principles, traditional, historic, or aesthetic rationales cannot justify a BFOQ. Thus, the preference of co-workers or customers does not justify a gender-based distinction.[49]

Is sex a BFOQ for police work?

No.[50] Women can, and do, perform effectively as police officers. Moreover, even if studies conclusively determined that women officers as a class were less effective than men, women officers must be judged on an individual rather than group basis.[51]

Are laws designed to "protect" women in police work valid?

Probably not. Over the years, state legislatures have enacted laws restricting the hours that women may work, the types of jobs to which they may be assigned, and other conditions of employment. Many such laws have been challenged and held either unconstitutional or in violation of federal or state laws forbidding sex discrimination.[52] The EEOC guidelines do not regard such laws as justifying otherwise invalid sex differentiation.[53] In order to meet the BFOQ test, any such laws must be shown to rest on business necessity.

Can women be excluded from higher-risk police jobs?

Usually not. In *Owens* v. *Brown*,[54] a federal district court invalidated a statute that prohibited the Navy from assigning female personnel to sea. The court found that the exclusion was not based on any studied evaluation of capabilities; nor was there proof that women lacked the "native" ability to perform competently on board. In short, the statutory prohibition was not substantially related to the achievement of important objectives. Rather, the "rationale" underlying the prohibition was no more than a presumption about "masculine traditions"—clearly invalid under the Constitution and Title VII.

By analogy, women could not be excluded from higher-risk police jobs unless narrowly drawn and solidly grounded reasons were proffered in support of the restriction. Generalized arguments about the need to maintain "police preparedness," or the supposed greater "efficiency of special [male] squads," will not do. If the department demonstrated, however, that the assignment of women to higher-risk positions created actual security problems, or posed realistic dangers of violence, then their exclusion would be valid under *Dothard* v. *Rawlinson*.[55]

Is pregnancy a bar to police work?

Not in the earlier months of pregnancy, but probably in the later months.

In 1978, Title VII was amended to prohibit employment discrimination "because of or on the basis of pregnancy, childbirth, or related medical conditions." [56] Accordingly, pregnant police officers cannot be treated differently from other officers in any respect, unless not being pregnant is a BFOQ and justified by business necessity. Moreover, mere assertions that pregnant women or mothers are unfit because of higher absentee rates, or prone to stress and "preoccupation," are insufficient.[57]

One justification for barring pregnant police officers is physical incapacity to do the job. In the later months of pregnancy an officer can be ordered to assume lighter police duties (or possibly take leave) if found unfit to patrol or use and defend against physical force.[58] Furthermore, although courts did not develop this concept in the context of Title VII, it is judicially recognized that during the last three months of pregnancy, the state has an interest in preserving the potential life of the fetus.[59] A police department that determines upon competent medical evidence that police work threatens a viable fetus would be justified in ordering the transfer of an officer during the last trimester of pregnancy.

In apparent recognition of these principles, the New York City Police Department issued the following interim order with regard to pregnant police officers.

Subject: DISABILITY DUE TO PREGNANCY AND PREGNANCY RELATED LEAVE

1. Pregnancy, for employment purposes, must be regarded in the same manner as any other disability when it interferes with an employee's capacity to perform.

2. Consequently, a pregnant member of the service will be expected to perform that kind of duty which she is capable of in light of her particular condition. When said member is incapacitated and unable to perform her assigned duties, she will report sick in accordance with Patrol Guide procedure.

3. During the period of sick report both before and after delivery, such member will be under the medical supervision of her assigned District Surgeon. She will be accorded the same privileges and be subject to the same restrictions as any other member of the service on sick report.

4. District Surgeons will decide when the member should be returned to duty and whether she should be placed on restricted duty both pre- and post-delivery. Such decisions will be made after consulta-

tion with the member's private physician and the Chief Surgeon, where appropriate.

5. Maternity leave for members of the service is abolished. A member who is determined to be fit for duty (either full or restricted) yet wishes additional time off before or after confinement may use accrued leave or make application for unpaid leave in accordance with the authorized leave provisions. If the requested leave is for thirty (30) days or more, the provisions of [an applicable order control].

6. Any provision of the Department Manual or other directive of the department in conflict with this order is suspended.[60]

The New York City guidelines may serve as a model for other departments.

Does Title VII's 1978 amendment cover all pregnant employees?

Almost all. The 1978 amendment prohibiting discrimination based on pregnancy became effective on October 31, 1978. If a collective bargaining agreement in effect on that date did not comport with the amendment, the amendment becomes effective at the expiration of that agreement.[61] Accordingly, all employees should soon be protected by the amendment.

Even in cases where the Title VII amendment is not yet in effect, a pregnant officer may not be compelled to take maternity leave unless an individual determination is made of her inability to perform police work.[62] In *United States* v. *City of Philadelphia,* the Court of Appeals for the Third Circuit ordered the reinstatement of a policewoman who was fired solely because she was pregnant.[63] The court found that the officer was merely—and impermissibly—presumed to be unfit.[64] In the later months of pregnancy, however, a department may permissibly dispense with an individual determination of fitness.

Are police officers automatically entitled to maternity leave?

Yes, during the period that the officer is actually disabled from working. If an employer denied sick leave for this period of disability while granting it for other illnesses unrelated to childbirth, the employer would violate Title VII's proscription against discrimination based on pregnancy and childbirth.[65]

As to the period when the officer is no longer disabled from working, there is no clear answer whether leave must be granted. The police officer should refer to federal, state, and local law in her jurisdiction. In Massachusetts, for example, an employee is entitled by statute to an eight-week maternity leave without pay.[66] And as the Massachusetts Supreme Judicial Court ruled in *School Committee of Braintree* v. *Massachusetts Commission Against Discrimination,* the employee cannot be denied *accrued* sick pay during that period of leave.[67] Furthermore, since Title VII prohibits "discrimination . . . based on childbirth," an employer who establishes a pattern—albeit informally—of granting employees leaves of absence without pay could not deny such leaves when requested for the purpose of childbearing.

Can a police officer use accrued sick leave during absence for maternity?

Probably. Although not many courts have ruled on the question, in *School Committee of Braintree,*[68] Massachusetts' highest court held that an employer's denial of accumulated sick leave to employees on long-term leaves for maternity- or pregnancy-related disabilities constituted unlawful sex discrimination:

Unlike leaves of other kinds, maternity leave possesses an essential character of being medically necessary. During several weeks of maternity leave a woman, by necessity, is physically disabled and incapable of performing her job. No comparable situation exists with respect to men. . . .

Accordingly, we think that the school committee's purportedly sex-neutral rules, which bar use of sick leave during all extended leaves of absence, visibly operate to the particular disadvantage of women. Since we are also of the opinion that this effect could not reasonably have escaped [the school committee's] attention, we believe that the commission could properly find that the school committee's policies are pretexts, designed, at least in part, to deny women access to accrued sick leave benefits.[69]

May a police officer be denied a promotion or accumulated seniority based on her taking maternity leave?

No. This practice is impermissible under the 1978 amendment to Title VII, as well as under the Supreme Court's decision in *National Gas Co.* v. *Satty,*[70] unless justified by business necessity. Moreover, it is difficult to conceive of any business necessity that would justify these burdens on officers back on the job.

Do male officers have a right to paternity leave?

Court decisions under the 1978 amendments are few, so this question remains unanswered. Under one reading of Title VII, discrimination based on paternity is unlawful, since Title VII prohibits "discrimination . . . based on childbirth."

Must officers receive health and medical benefits for their pregnancy and childbirth?

Yes, once the 1978 amendment to Title VII becomes effective. For those not yet protected by this amendment, medical coverage is not required under federal law,[71] but may be required under state human-rights or equal-employment statutes.[72]

Are unmarried mothers protected against denial of pregnancy-related leaves and benefits?

Yes. Title VII by its terms does not make a distinction based upon the marital status of the mother. Additionally, an evolving line of cases requires that employees not be penalized for nontraditional sexual conduct unless a connection is demonstrated between that conduct and impaired job effectiveness.[73] These cases and other privacy issues are discussed in detail in Chapter V.

Does Title VII's prohibition against discrimination based on pregnancy include the termination of pregnancy by abortion?

No. Federal law does not require that employers pay health-insurance benefits for termination of pregnancy by abortion, except where the life of the woman would be endangered if the fetus were carried to term, or if medical complications arose from the abortion.[74] Medical coverage for abortion may be sought via collective-bargaining agreements, private insurance plans, or state legislation.

Are state statutes that prohibit insurance coverage of abortions valid?

There is no clear answer.

Some states, such as Massachusetts, disallow state employees' medical insurance plans from covering abortions, except if certified by a panel of approved physicians as necessary to prevent the death of the pregnant woman.[75] Even in cases of incest or rape, promptly reported, insurance coverage is prohibited. Thus, even though most other medical procedures are covered by insurance, policewomen in Massachusetts must fund the procedure of abortion. It is unclear whether the Massachusetts scheme is valid. Neither the Constitution nor Title VII has been interpreted to prohibit such statutes.[76] By contrast, Massachusetts cases have held that the singling out of a sex-specific procedure for differential treatment constitutes unlawful discrimination under state statutes.[77] Under this reasoning, the Massachusetts scheme would be invalid.

Is motherhood a bar to police work?

No, practically speaking. In *Phillips* v. *Martin Marietta Corp.*,[78] the Supreme Court held that an employer may not refuse to consider applications from women with pre-school children while accepting applications from men with preschool children. The Court ruled, "The existence of such conflicting family obligations, if demonstratively more relevant to job performance for a woman than for a man, could arguably be a basis for [excluding mothers]. . . . But that is a matter of evidence." [79]

Is "parenting" on the job allowed?

Maybe. In January 1979 Linda Eaton, a firefighter in Iowa City, Iowa, asked permission to breast-feed her four-month-old son during duty hours. The fire chief and the city refused, saying it would violate a rule against "regularly scheduled family visits" at the firehouse. Eaton breast-fed her son anyway, and was suspended twice. The State Civil Rights Commission heard the case, and decided that the city discriminated against Eaton. The case is now in the courts.[80]

Are police officers protected from sexual harassment on the job?

Yes. The federal appellate courts agree that physical or verbal sexual harassment is unlawful under Title VII when it is the basis of an employment decision such as hiring, promotion, transfer, and firing.[81] Once a response to an unwelcome sexual advance provokes a favorable or unfavorable job evaluation, or a grant or denial of a promotion, [82] or a firing,[83] or the "abolishing of an employment position" [84]—and the employer approves of or acquiesces in such practice [85]—a Title VII violation is established.[86] An employer who receives a complaint has a duty to investigate the circumstances before rubber-stamping a supervisor's adverse treatment of an employee who refused sexual advances.[87] These rules can be used by men against the demands of female or homosexual supervisors, but *not* against a bisexual supervisor, because then there would be no gender-based discrimination.[88]

Under EEOC regulations that became effective in 1980, sexual harassment, whether physical or verbal, may be unlawful even if there is no immediate employment reprisal. The new regulations protect against an unwelcome sexual advance if it has the purpose or effect of unreasonably interfering with an individual's work performance or of creating an intimidating, hostile, or offensive working environment.[89] An employer (here, the police department or locality) is responsible for the acts of its supervisors and administrators, regardless of authorization or knowledge. The department may also be liable for the acts of fellow officers in those instances where superiors knew or should have known of the conduct, unless immediate and appropriate corrective action is taken.[90] However, a random unwelcome approach by a peer, unknown and unknowable to the employer, is not remediable under Title VII.

As stated above, a sexual advance is not prohibited under Title VII if it does not result in an employment reprisal or an impaired work environment. The reason is that Title VII protects against discrimination only in the "terms and conditions" of employment. Unwelcome advances alone might be a basis for a state tort suit. Moreover, as a practical matter, persistent, unsought sexual overtures are likely to interfere with work environment and come to the attention of the employer, thereby falling within the reach of Title VII.

Can a department require a greater contribution from women for employment benefits such as pensions and annuities?

No. In *Los Angeles Department of Water and Power* v. *Manhart,* the Supreme Court ruled that a pension plan which requires greater contributions from women employees violates Title VII.[91]

In *Manhart* the Court acknowledged the greater longevity of women—and the resultant anticipated receipt of higher benefits over a lifetime. The Court ruled, however, that Title VII requires that employers focus on employees as individuals and not classes: accordingly, actuarial statistics that are valid for women as a group may not compensate for unfairness to the individual woman.

The *Manhart* decision is a legal milestone. It rejects the notion that women (and minorities) may be treated as components of a group, and reaffirms the precept that generalizations, albeit true, are not necessarily right, nor just.

May differing mortality tables justify different pension payouts to men and women officers?

Probably not. Although the *Manhart* decision did not treat this question, its rationale answers it. Women may not receive lower monthly pension or annuity payments than men, despite their admittedly greater life expectancy, because women must be assessed as individuals and not as a class. Indeed, at least three courts have held that the payment of lower monthly retirement benefits to women, based upon separate mortality tables, is unlawful.[92]

What must an officer prove in a sex-discrimination charge?

The employee charging sex discrimination in hiring or promotion must establish that he or she was qualified for the position, that despite these qualifications the application was rejected, and that the agency thereafter continued to seek applicants with similar qualifications. Proof of the disproportionate effect of a requirement upon women (or men) (such as height and weight regulations) will, as we have discussed, shift the burden of proof to the department.[93]

What remedies are available when unlawful sex discrimination has been proved?

As with race and age discrimination, a successful complainant will be entitled to be hired, rehired, or promoted and thus put where he or she would have been if not for the unlawful discrimination. An injunction may also be issued, forbidding the repetition or continuation of the unlawful policy or practice. The remedy of back pay from the department or the city is also available to offset the effects of discrimination.[94] Under Title VII, back pay may be recovered for two years prior to the filing of a claim with the EEOC or a suit in court. Under the Equal Pay Act, the normal limit on back pay is also two years, although a complainant may recover back pay for a period up to three years if the employer's violation was willful.

May strict numerical hiring be ordered as a remedy in sex-discrimination cases?

Yes. If a court finds that there has been a pattern of past discrimination against either sex, and that less drastic measures would not suffice, it may order that a percentage of new employees be drawn from the disadvantaged sex. In *United States* v. *City of Philadelphia*,[95] the Third Circuit Court of Appeals affirmed a district court order for the hiring of one hundred women for the upcoming 470 vacancies in the police force. The Third Circuit also affirmed an order approving the overall hiring of 20 percent women officers. This order was issued early in the lawsuit where no conclusive judicial finding of sex-based discrimination had yet been made, but where a strong likelihood existed of discrimination by the Philadelphia police department, the third largest in the nation. After a trial in the case in 1979, the city was permanently enjoined from discriminating on the basis of sex. A subsequent order consented to by the Philadelphia department granted the most extensive relief on behalf of women ever ordered in a sex-discrimination suit against a police department. The decree required the city to hire women for 30 percent of the next 2,670 police officer vacancies and to promote women to the next sixteen detective openings and the next seventeen sergeant vacancies. The department also agreed to establish a program to recruit women officers and to assign them throughout the city and to special police units. The department also granted back-pay awards of up to $22,488 to individual officers, totaling $700,000 paid to ninety-six complainants.

May the department voluntarily adopt a preference favoring women in its hiring policies?

Perhaps. Where there has been a background of discrimination against women or underrepresentation of women in the police force, and where no program other than preferential hiring can remedy the imbalance, a voluntary preference would seem valid.[96] At the least, departments may take the factor of gender into consideration in hiring.[97]

NOTES

1. 42 U.S.C. §§2000e to 2000e-17 (1976).
2. 42 U.S.C. §1983 (1976); see 42 U.S.C. §1981 (1976).
3. Washington v. Davis, 426 U.S. 229 (1976). Allen v. City of Mobile, 464 F. Supp. 433 (S.D. Ala. 1978). See Albermarle Paper Co. v. Moody, 422 U.S. 405 (1975); Firefighters Institute for Racial Equality v. City of St. Louis, 616 F.2d 350 (8th Cir. 1980), petition for cert. filed, 49 U.S.L.W. 3014 (U.S. July 8, 1980) (No. 80-29); Ensley Branch v. Seibels, 22 Fair Empl. Prac. Cas. 1207, 48 U.S.L.W. 2774 (5th Cir. May 8, 1980); United States v. City of Chicago, 549 F.2d 415 (7th Cir.), cert. denied, 434 U.S. 875 (1977). Cf. Harless v. Duck, 22 Fair Empl. Prac. Cas. 1073 (6th Cir. 1980), cert. denied, 49 U.S.L.W. 3249 (U.S. Oct. 6, 1980) (No. 80-86) (oral interviews).
4. Raab, Police Strength and Racial Mix Await Decisions in Court Battle, New York Times, Jan. 30, 1980, at B1, col. 1; B4, cols. 1 & 2 (hereinafter Racial Mix, New York Times).
5. Rate of Failure Grows on Other Police Tests, New York Times, Jan. 30, 1980, at B4, col. 3.
6. See Washington v. Davis, 426 U.S. 229 (1976); Hardy

v. Stumpf, 21 Cal. 3d 1, 145 Cal. Rptr. 176, 576 P.2d 1342 (1978).

7. Washington v. Davis, 426 U.S. 229 (1976).

8. In the housing and free-speech areas, the Supreme Court has suggested that government action "motivated in part by a racially discriminatory purpose" can be excused if the government shows "that the same decision would have resulted even had the impermissible purpose not been considered." Arlington Heights v. Metropolitan Hous. Dev. Corp., 429 U.S. 252, 270-71 n. 21 (1977); Mount Healthy City Bd. of Educ. v. Doyle, 429 U.S. 274, 287 (1977). It is unclear whether this defense is available in employment cases.

9. Allen v. City of Mobile, 464 F. Supp. 433 (S.D. Ala. 1978). *Accord,* Albermarle Paper Co. v. Moody, 422 U.S. 405, 425 (1975); United States v. City of Chicago, 573 F.2d 416, 421 (7th Cir. 1978). *Cf.* Texas Dep't of Community Affairs v. Burdine, 48 U.S.L.W. 3820 (U.S. June 16, 1980) (No. 79–1764) (granting petition for certiorari), *reviewing* 608 F.2d 563 (5th Cir. 1979).

10. EEOC Guidelines, 29 C.F.R. §1607.3A (1979).

11. *See* 47 U.S.L.W. 2142 (Aug. 29, 1978).

12. Guardians Ass'n v. Civil Serv. Comm'n, 21 Fair Empl. Prac. Cas. 1467 (S.D.N.Y. 1980) *appeal filed* (2d Cir). *See also* Guardians Ass'n v. Civil Serv. Comm'n, 466 F. Supp. 1273 (S.D.N.Y. 1979), *aff'd in part,* 23 Fair Empl. Prac. Cas. 677 (2d Cir. July 15, 1980); *Racial Mix,* New York Times, *supra* note 4.

13. *Id.*

14. Answers: 1(B); 2(B); 3(C); 4(B).

15. Guardians Ass'n v. Civil Serv. Comm'n, 21 Fair Empl. Prac. Cas. at 1472.

16. *Racial Mix,* New York Times, *supra* note 4.

17. County of Los Angeles v. Davis, 47 U.S.L.W. 4317 (U.S. 1978) (dismissing appeal from 566 F.2d 1334 (9th Cir. 1977) on grounds of mootness).

18. 29 C.F.R. §1607.3 (1979), *discussed in* Allen v. City of Mobile, 464 F. Supp. 433 (S.D. Ala. 1978). *See* cases cited in note 3 *supra.*

19. 29 C.F.R. §1607.5 (1979).

20. Guardians Ass'n v. Civil Serv. Comm'n, 23 Fair Empl. Prac. Cas. 677, 683–88 (2d Cir. July 25, 1980), *aff'g in relevant part,* 466 F. Supp. 1273 (S.D.N.Y. 1979). *See* cases cited in note 3 *supra.*

21. Craig v. County of Los Angeles, 626 F.2d 659 (9th Cir. 1980); Harless v. Duck, 22 Fair Empl. Prac. Cas. 1073 (6th Cir. 1980); cert. denied, 49 U.S.L.W. 3249 (U.S. Oct. 6, 1980) (No. 80–86); Blake v. City of Los Angeles, 595 F.2d 1367 (9th Cir. 1979), cert. denied, 100 S. Ct. 1865 (1980).

22. Racial Mix, New York Times, supra, note 4. See Craig v. County of Los Angeles, 626 F.2d 659 (9th Cir. 1980); United States v. Virginia, 620 F.2d 1018, 1024 (4th Cir. 1980).

23. See Firefighters Inst. v. City of St. Louis, 588 F.2d 235 (8th Cir. 1978), cert. denied, 442 U.S. 904 (1979); United States v. City of Philadelphia, 573 F.2d 802 (3d Cir.), cert. denied, 439 U.S. 830 (1978); Allen v. City of Mobile, 464 F. Supp. 433, 441 (S.D. Ala. 1978).

24. United States v. City of Philadelphia, 573 F.2d 802 (3d Cir.), cert. denied, 439 U.S. 830 (1978). Association against Discrimination in Employment v. City of Bridgeport, 479 F. Supp. 101, 112–13 (D. Conn. 1979). See R. O'Neil, The Rights of Government Employees 135 (1978).

25. Guardians Ass'n v. Civil Serv. Comm'n, 21 Fair Empl. Prac. Cas. 1467 (S.D.N.Y. 1980), appeal filed (2d Cir.). O'Neil, supra note 24, at 135. Racial Mix, New York Times, supra note 4.

26. New York Times, Aug. 8, 1980, at A1, col. 3; Racial Mix, New York Times, supra note 4.

27. Cf. Fullilove v. Klutznick, 48 U.S.L.W. 4979 (U.S. 1979), aff'g 584 F.2d 600 (2d Cir. 1978).

28. 442 U.S. 193 (1979).

29. 438 U.S. 265 (1978).

30. Association against Discrimination in Employment v. City of Bridgeport, 479 F. Supp. 101 (D. Conn. 1979). See Detroit Police Officers Ass'n v. Young, 608 F.2d 671 (6th Cir. 1979), petition for cert. filed, 48 U.S.L.W. 3558 (U.S. Feb. 26, 1980) (No. 79–1080); Price v. Civil Serv. Comm'n, 48 U.S.L.W. 2538 (Cal. Jan. 25, 1980). Cf. Electrical Workers, Local No. 35 v. City of Hartford, 48 U.S.L.W. (2d Cir. June 13, 1980) (upheld city's affirmative action plan for construction industry based on city council finding of past and present discrimination).

31. See EEOC Guidelines on Affirmative Action dated Dec. 19, 1978, 29 C.F.R. §§1607.13, 1607.17 (1979), discussed at 47 U.S.L.W. 2390.

32. *See id.*
33. 479 F. Supp. 101 (D. Conn. 1979), *aff'g* 47 U.S.L.W. 2124 (D. Conn. July 31, 1978).
34. In Minnick v. California Dep't of Corrections, 48 U.S.L.W. 3855 (U.S. July 2, 1980) (No. 79–1213) (granting petition for certiorari), the Supreme Court agreed to review the issue whether a state agency may voluntarily establish promotion and transfer preferences for women and minorities in the absence of prior intentional discrimination and based solely on the disparate impact of past hiring practices.
35. *See Racial Mix,* New York Times, *supra* note 4.
36. 608 F.2d 671 (6th Cir. 1979), *rev'g* 446 F. Supp. 979 (E.D. Mich. 1978), *petition for cert. filed,* 48 U.S.L.W. 3558 (U.S. Feb. 26, 1980) (No. 79–1080). *Accord,* Price v. Civil Serv. Comm'n, 48 U.S.L.W. 2538 (Cal. Jan. 25, 1980). *See* Baker v. Detroit, 49 U.S.L.W. 2387 (E.D. Mich. Nov. 17, 1980). *See also* Pettinaro Construction Co. v. Delaware Auth. for Regional Transit, 49 U.S.L.W. 2320 (D. Mass. Sept. 22, 1980).
37. Detroit Police Officers Ass'n v. Young, 608 F.2d 671 (6th Cir. 1979), *petition for cert. filed,* 48 U.S.L.W. 3558 (U.S. Feb. 26, 1980) (No. 79–1080). *See* Price v. Civil Serv. Comm'n, 48 U.S.L.W. 2538 (Cal. Jan. 25, 1980).
38. EEOC Guidelines on Affirmative Action dated Dec. 19, 1978, 29 C.F.R. §§1607.13, 1607.17 (1979), *discussed at* 47 U.S.L.W. 2390.
39. 42 U.S.C. §§2000e to 2000e–17 (1976).
40. *E.g.,* United States v. City of Philadelphia, 573 F.2d 802 (3d Cir.), *cert. denied,* 439 U.S. 830 (1978).
41. 42 U.S.C. §2000e–2(e) (1976).
42. 29 U.S.C. §206 (1976).
43. *Id.* §206(d).
44. 42 U.S.C. §1983 (1976).
45. MASS. GEN. LAWS ANN. ch. 1149, §105A (West 1971).
46. 433 U.S. 321, 333–34 (1977).
47. Diaz v. Pan American World Airways, 442 F.2d 385, 388 (5th Cir.), *cert. denied,* 404 U.S. 950 (1971); Weeks v. Southern Bell Tel. & Tel. Co., 408 F.2d 228, 235 (5th Cir. 1969).
48. 29 C.F.R. §1604 (1979).
49. *Id.* §1604.2.
50. United States v. City of Philadelphia, 573 F.2d 802 (3d Cir.), *cert. denied,* 439 U.S. 830 (1978). *See* McKer-

nan v. Town of Framingham, Mass. Lawyers Weekly No. 137 (MCAD 1979).

51. *See* cases cited notes 47 and 50 *supra. Cf.* Los Angeles Department of Water & Power v. Manhart, 434 U.S. 815 (1978); Peters v. Wayne State Univ., 48 U.S.L.W. 2278 (E.D. Mich. Sept. 25, 1979).

52. *E.g.,* Richards v. Griffith Rubber Mills, 300 F. Supp. 338 (D. Ore. 1969). *See* O'NEIL, *supra* note 24, at 143.

53. 29 C.F.R. §1604.2(b) (1979).

54. 455 F. Supp. 291 (D. Colo. 1978).

55. 433 U.S. at 335–37. In Rostker v. Goldberg, 49 U.S.L.W. 3401 (U.S. Dec. 1, 1980) (No. 80–251) (granting petition for certiorari), the Supreme Court agreed to decide whether the registration of males only for possible involuntary induction into the armed services discriminates unlawfully against men in violation of the Fifth Amendment.

56. Act of Oct. 31, 1978, Pub. L. No. 95–555, 92 Stat. 2076 (codified at 42 U.S.C. §2000e–2).

57. *See In re* Airline Cases, 582 F.2d 1142 (7th Cir. 1978), *petition for cert. filed,* 47 U.S.L.W. 3700 (U.S. Apr. 11, 1979) (No. 78–1549).

58. *See* Burwell v. Eastern Air Lines, 49 U.S.L.W. 2180 (4th Cir. Aug. 29, 1980) (en banc) (unfit only after thirteenth week); *In re* National Airlines, 434 F. Supp. 269 (S.D. Fla. 1977) (unfit only after twentieth week). *But cf.* Pan American Airways, —— F.2d —— (9th Cir. 1980) (Wash. Post, Dec. 25, 1980) (unfit as soon as flight attendant becomes aware of pregnancy).

59. Roe v. Wade, 410 U.S. 113, 163–65 (1973).

60. New York City Police Department Interim Order No. 45 (November 30, 1978) (citations omitted).

61. Act of Oct. 31, 1978, Pub. L. No. 95–555, 92 Stat. 2076 (codified at 42 U.S.C. §2000e–2).

62. Cleveland Bd. of Educ. v. LaFleur, 414 U.S. 632 (1974) (applying due-process clause of Fourteenth Amendment).

63. 573 F.2d 802 (3d Cir.), *cert. denied,* 439 U.S. 830 (1978).

64. *Accord,* United Air Lines v. State Human Rights Appeal Bd., 61 App. Div. 2d 1010, 402 N.Y.S. 2d 630 (2d Dep't), *cert. denied,* 439 U.S. 982 (1978) (airline's policy of mandatory, unpaid pregnancy leave violates state anti-discrimination law). *See* cases cited *supra* note 58.

65. *See* 42 U.S.C. §2000e–2 (1976).

66. MASS. GEN. LAWS ANN. ch. 149, §105D (West Supp. 1979).

67. 1979 Mass. Adv. Sh. 543, 368 N.E.2d 1251 (1979).

68. 1979 Mass. Adv. Sh. 543, 368 N.E.2d 1251 (1979).

69. *Id.* at 552–53.

70. 434 U.S. 136 (1977).

71. General Elec. Co. v. Gilbert, 429 U.S. 125 (1976); Geduldig v. Aiello, 417 U.S. 484 (1974).

72. N.Y. EXEC. LAW, art. 15 (McKinney 1972 & McKinney Supp. 1979); Brooklyn Union Gas Co. v. State Human Rights Appeal Bd., 41 N.Y.2d 84, 359 N.E.2d 393, 390 N.Y.S.2d 884 (1976); Westinghouse Elec. Corp. v. State Human Rights Appeal Bd., 60 App. Div. 2d 943, 401 N.Y.S.2d 597 (3d Dep't 1978); Anderson v. Upper Bucks County Area Vocational Tech. School, 30 Pa. Comm. Ct. 103, 373 A.2d 126 (1977), *interpreting* 43 Pa. Cons. Stat. Ann. §955(a) (Purdon Supp. 1979); 1977 ORE. LAWS, ch. 330, §2, *amending* ORE. REV. STAT. §659.029–.030 (1977).

73. Andrews v. Drew Mun. Separate School Dist., 507 F.2d 611 (5th Cir. 1975), *cert. dismissed as improvidently granted*, 425 U.S. 559 (1976) (teachers' aides); Drake v. Covington County Bd. of Educ., 371 F. Supp. 974 (M.D. Ala. 1974) (teacher).

74. Act of Oct. 31, 1978, Pub. L. No. 95–555, 92 Stat. 2076 (codified at 42 U.S.C. §2000e).

75. MASS. GEN. LAWS ANN. ch. 32A, §4 (West Supp. 1980).

76. General Elec. Co. v. Gilbert, 429 U.S. 125 (1976); Geduldig v. Aiello, 417 U.S. 484 (1974). *See* Maher v. Roe, 432 U.S. 464 (1977); Beal v. Doe, 432 U.S. 438 (1977).

77. *See* Massachusetts Elec. Co. v. Massachusetts Comm'n against Discrimination, 1978 Mass. Adv. Sh. 1189, 375 N.E.2d 1192 (1978). *Cf.* Framingham Clinic, Inc. v. Selectmen of Southborough, 373 Mass. 279, 367 N.E.2d 606 (1977).

78. 400 U.S. 542 (1971).

79. *Id.* at 544.

80. Boston Globe, Mar. 1, 1979, at 4, col. 1 (Names . . . Faces).

81. *See, e.g.,* Miller v. Bank of America, 600 F.2d 211, 213 (9th Cir. 1979); Tomkins v. Public Serv. Elec. & Gas Co., 568 F.2d 1044 (3d Cir. 1977); Barnes v. Costle, 561

F.2d 983 (D.C. Cir. 1977); Garber v. Saxon Business Prod., Inc., 552 F.2d 1032 (4th Cir. 1977). *But see* Cordes v. County of Yavapai, 17 Fair Empl. Prac. Cas. 1224 (D. Ariz. 1978); Corne v. Bausch & Lomb, Inc., 390 F. Supp. 161 (D. Ariz. 1975), *rev'd and remanded on other grounds*, 15 Fair Empl. Prac. Cas. 1370 (9th Cir. 1977). *See also* 45 Fed. Reg. 74676, 25024 (1980) (Guidelines on Discrimination Because of Sexual Harassment) (to be codified at 29 C.F.R. §1604.11). *See generally* Comment, 1979 Ann. Survey Am. L. 446; Comment, *Sexual Harassment and Title VII*, 51 N.Y.U.L. REV. 148 (1976).

82. Tomkins v. Public Serv. Elec. & Gas Co., 568 F.2d at 1048.

83. Garber v. Saxon Business Prod., Inc. 552 F.2d 1032 (4th Cir. 1977).

84. Barnes v. Costle, 561 F.2d at 990-91.

85. Garber v. Saxon Business Prod., Inc., 552 F.2d at 1032. Harmon v. San Diego County, 477 F. Supp. 1084 (S.D. Cal. 1979) (governmental entity responsible for acts by individuals in their respective capacities).

86. Tomkins v. Public Serv. Elec. & Gas Co., 568 F.2d at 1048–49; Barnes v. Costle, 561 F.2d at 993.

87. Stringer v. Dep't of Community Affairs, 446 F. Supp. 704, 705 (M.D. Pa. 1978).

88. Tomkins v. Public Serv. Elec. & Gas Co., 568 F.2d at 1047 n. 4; Barnes v. Costle, 561 F.2d at 990 & n. 55.

89. 45 Fed. Reg. 74676, 25024 (1980) (to be codified at 29 C.F.R. §1604.11). *See* 49 U.S.L.W. 2221 (Sept. 11, 1980).

90. *Id.* at 25025 (to be codified at 29 C.F.R. §1604.11(d)).

91. 434 U.S. 815 (1978).

92. Colby College v. EEOC, 589 F.2d 1139 (1st Cir. 1979). Peters v. Wayne State Univ., 48 U.S.L.W. 2278 (E.D. Mich. Sept. 25, 1979). Reilly v. Robertson, 266 Ind. 29, *cert. denied*, 434 U.S. 825 (1977).

93. *See* Allen v. City of Mobile, 464 F. Supp. 433 (S.D. Ala. 1979), *citing* Albemarle Paper Co. v. Moody, 422 U.S. 405 (1975).

94. Fitzpatrick v. Bitzer, 427 U.S. 445 (1976).

95. 573 F.2d 802 (3d Cir.), *cert. denied*, 439 U.S. 830 (1978).

96. *See* Minnick v. California Dep't of Corrections, 95 Cal. App. 3d 506, 48 U.S.L.W. 2128 (1979) (upholding department of corrections' preferential promotion and trans-

fer plan in the absence of past proven discrimination), *petition for cert. granted,* 48 U.S.L.W. 3855 (U.S. July 2, 1980) (No. 79–1213). *Cf.* Detroit Police Officers Ass'n v. Young, 608 F.2d 671 (6th Cir. 1979), *petition for cert. filed,* 48 U.S.L.W. 3558 (U.S. Feb. 26, 1980).
97. Regents of Univ. of Cal. v. Bakke, 438 U.S. 265 (1978).

III

First Amendment Rights

When Frank Serpico blew the whistle on corruption in the New York City Police Department several years ago, a movie was made about his story. It showed that ostracism and physical threats were his reward for revealing rampant, illegal police practices. While future whistleblowers may not attract Hollywood's attention, the protection accorded police officers who speak out against their superiors or against department practices has recently been enhanced. A Third Circuit opinion by Judge Garth upheld the free-speech rights of a Newark, New Jersey, police officer whom the department sought to punish for criticizing his superiors. Future Frank Serpicos may still not win popularity contests within police departments, but they will be protected from arbitrary and vindictive reprisals.

Moreover, on the federal level, the Civil Service Reform Act of 1978 now explicitly protects whistleblowers in the Federal Bureau of Investigation. If an agent impugns his colleagues or superiors, they may not want to lunch with him, but they cannot take personnel action against him.

This chapter will examine police officers' First Amendment rights both on duty and off duty. Generally, a police officer's freedom of activity is greater off duty, although off-duty activity that compromises an officer's ability to do the job is more likely to be regulable than activity that relates less directly to competence. Many restrictions on First Amendment rights affect police officers in the same way that they affect public employees generally. In those instances another ACLU handbook, Robert O'Neil's *The Rights of Government Employees* (New York: Avon

69

Books, 1978) will be relied on for a discussion of the relevant rights.

May a police officer be required to take an oath of allegiance?

Yes. The type of oath that may be required is an affirmation that a police officer "will uphold and defend the Constitution of the United States of America and the Constitution of [the state] and that [he or she] will oppose the overthrow of the government of the United States of America or of [the state] by force, violence or by any illegal or unconstitutional method." [1] Because public employees generally can be required to make such a pledge, the case is surely stronger for requiring such an oath from those responsible for enforcing laws and for protecting the country or a state from public disorder and unlawful overthrow.

May police officers be required to affirm political beliefs?

Only in a most limited fashion.

Robert O'Neil writes, "In general, no oath broader than the oath of allegiance may be required of an applicant for public employment." [2] As examples of impermissible oaths, he points to state laws requiring public employees to "promote respect for the flag and [for federal and state] institutions . . . , reverence for law and order and undivided allegiance to the government." [3] The Supreme Court has invalidated such oaths as too vague and as overbroad. Similarly, demanding that public employees disavow membership in "subversive organizations" has been invalidated as unduly vague and as infringing on the associational rights of those who belong to such a group, but who do not engage in unlawful activity. [4]

In the case of police officers, however, certain very limited avowals of political belief may be required in light of *Kelley* v. *Johnson.* [5] One of the rationales underlying the *Kelley* decision, which upheld a departmental grooming code, included the inculcation of esprit de corps. If a grooming code inculcates such spirit, a flag salute requirement certainly does. Indeed, in *Kelley* the Supreme Court expressly referred to the duty to salute as one element of the overall requirement of discipline. [6] Thus, it is not difficult to imagine the Supreme Court upholding a specific and precise requirement that police officers salute the flag at appropriate times. In other contexts, this act has been considered tantamount to an avowal of political belief.[7] Moreover, lower courts have upheld the authority of police departments to require officers to wear American flag patches on their uniforms.[8]

May a police officer be punished for disavowing certain political beliefs?

Not in most circumstances.

In the recent case of *Wooley* v. *Maynard,* the Supreme Court upheld the right of a Jehovah's Witness to cover up the slogan "Live Free or Die" on his New Hampshire license plates.[9] By so doing, the Court recognized his right to be free from the coerced avowal of the political belief inherent in the slogan. None of the reasons underlying *Kelley* v. *Johnson* warrants different treatment for police officers who might choose to cover up a similar slogan on their personal automobiles. Forbidding such an act would hardly make police officers more identifiable to the public; nor would it be likely to inculcate esprit de corps. Of course, a police department could prevent the covering of such a slogan on the license plates of official vehicles.

May an applicant for a position on a police force be required to disavow membership in a specific organization?

The rule for government employees generally is that a public employer may require a disclaimer limited to an individual's active membership in an organization which the member knows has illegal objectives and whose objectives the member specifically intends to promote. Thus, an applicant may not be asked simply if he is a card-carrying member of the Communist Party, the Ku Klux Klan, or the Nazi Party. He may be asked if he is an active member of an organization which incites its members to carry out unlawful acts and if so, whether he has a specific intent to promote the objectives of the organization.

The question then arises whether police officers may be treated differently from other public employees with respect to membership disclaimers. Arguably, the role of maintaining law and order is intolerably inconsistent with even inactive membership in a paramilitary organization, such as the Ku Klux Klan, which has a history of violence. One obvious problem is that the police officer might be reluctant to enforce the law against fellow members. However, because of its severe encroachment on First Amendment freedoms, inquiring into mere membership would probably be forbidden. On the other hand, paying annual dues to the KKK may be some evidence of active membership, knowledge of illegal aims, and specific intent to promote those aims. If that is added to other evidence and logical inferences from the evidence showing more than mere membership, a police department might make a case that an individual ought to be excluded from police work since the evidence indicates active membership with knowledge of an organization's illegal aims and with specific intent to promote those aims.[10]

How does the federal loyalty and security apparatus affect federal law-enforcement officials such as agents of the Federal Bureau of Investigation?

FBI agents, like other federal civil-service employees,[11] are required to take an oath of office professing loyalty to and support of the Constitution of the United States. In addition, within sixty days of accepting employment, an FBI agent is required to execute an affidavit swearing that he does not advocate the "overthrow of our constitutional form of government," that he is not "a member of an organization that he knows advocates the overthrow of our constitutional form of government," that he does not assert "the right to strike against the Government of the United States or the government of the District of Columbia" or participate in such strikes, and that he is not a "member of an organization of employees of the Government of the United States or of individuals employed by the government of the District of Columbia that he knows asserts the right to strike against the Government of the United States or the government of the District of Columbia."[12] Forbidding FBI agents to join organizations which advocate a right to strike may be unconstitutional, however.[13]

In addition, FBI agents, as employees of the Department of Justice, are subject to a federal statute that grants the Attorney General authority to suspend and ultimately to remove an FBI agent from continued employment "in the interests of national security." [14] However, the Supreme Court has limited the reach of the statute to persons in "sensitive" positions with a potential for adversely affecting national security.[15] In *Cole* v. *Young,* the dismissal of a food and drug inspector of the Department of Health, Education, and Welfare was invalidated since the requisite national-security determination was not made.[16]

There are no cases determining whether the position of an FBI agent constitutes a sensitive position within the meaning of *Cole* v. *Young.* The answer will probably depend on the tasks to which an individual agent is assigned or the information to which the agent has access. If he or she investigates garden-variety bank robberies, kidnapping, or drug-related crimes, the position would not be sensitive in the national-security sense. If, on the other hand, the agent were assigned, for example, to the prevention and detection of "espionage, sabotage, subversion, and other unlawful activities by or on behalf of foreign powers," [17] or to produce and disseminate foreign intelligence, counterintelligence and counterintelligence studies and reports," [18] then a court would be much more likely to conclude that the agent occupied a sensitive position. So too if the agent has access to national security information.

Robert O'Neil has succinctly outlined the procedure for loyalty checks on

> people being considered for or actually appointed to sensitive federal positions. The scope of the investigation depends on the sensitivity of the position, but will typically include at least a fingerprint check with the FBI . . . and inquiries to other law enforcement agencies, former employers, landlords, and perhaps other references. If evidence impugning the applicant's or employee's loyalty emerges during such an investigation, the agency may suspend the employee or even remove such a person by following the statutorily prescribed procedures.[19] . . . Probationary (i.e., nonpermanent) employees, who would be most commonly subject to the results of a security check, enjoy only the rather limited right to submit written statements to refute such charges and may not under

the general federal Civil Service law demand a hearing.[20] . . .

The range of information that may be considered in determining whether an applicant or employee poses any risk to the national security is quite broad. It may include law violations, drunkenness or drug addiction, mental illness, sexual deviation, and other conditions.[21] . . .

Finally, there are provisions restricting the reemployment of a person who is dismissed or denied employment for security reasons. Such a person may be rehired in the same or a different department only if the head of the department finds that such employment is clearly consistent with the interests of national security. In addition, the appointment of such a person to a different agency or department may be made only after the head of the new agency consults the Civil Service Commission, which may determine whether the person is eligible for employment in a department other than the original one.[22]

Are nonpolitical associations also protected by the Constitution? *

Yes. Although most suspect associations are political, nonpolitical association by police officers has also been the target of departmental regulation. Several years ago, the Baltimore Police Department rejected an applicant who revealed that he belonged to a nudist society. There was no indication that the applicant would refuse to wear clothes on the job or to enforce laws against indecent exposure. Nor was there any evidence of illegal activity on the part of the nudist group. Thus the federal court held that the applicant's First Amendment freedoms include "the right to associate with any person of one's choosing for the purpose of advocating and promoting legitimate, albeit controversial, political, social and economic views." [23] The police commissioner had failed to demonstrate any governmental interest that outweighed the strong associational interest of the applicant. While

---

* This and the following three questions and answers are adapted from Robert O'Neil's *The Rights of Government Employees* (New York: Avon Books, 1978).

such cases are rare outside the political context, the basic precepts apply equally to other forms of association.

Is the language of an oath significant? *

Yes. Many of the earlier Supreme Court cases turned on the vagueness and uncertainty of language, such as that of a Florida oath, which required employees to swear that they would not "lend aid, support, advise, counsel or influence to the Communist Party." [24] Later cases have also stressed the need for precision and clarity, especially because the exercise of First Amendment liberties might be "chilled" or discouraged by unclear or imprecise language.[25]

On the other hand, there may be such a thing as excessive precision. If a law is directed at a specific, named organization, and if it carries criminal penalties, it might violate another constitutional provision. A decade ago, the Supreme Court struck down an act of Congress that made it a crime for any officer of the Communist Party to serve as an officer of a labor union. While the government may have reason to protect unions from Communist influence, that goal could not be served by singling out a designated group of people. This was what the framers of the Constitution had in mind by forbidding "bills of attainder." [26] (A bill of attainder is a law [that applies either to named individuals or to easily ascertainable members of a group and imposes penalties on them without a judicial trial.]) Thus an oath focused *too* narrowly upon a particular named group or organization might be struck down for reasons quite different from those that involve loose and vague language.

May an applicant be required to forswear future political activity or affiliation? *

Constitutional protection for past or present political association applies with even greater force to the future. It is one thing to ask an applicant about groups to which he or she has belonged or now belongs; it is another and more hazardous matter to ask a person to agree for the indefinite future to steer clear of groups that may not even

* See footnote to preceding question.

exist and can at best be loosely described. Even in theory, the most that an applicant could be forced to forswear is knowing, active membership in illegal organizations with a specific intent to further those illegal aims. As a practical matter, it seems unlikely that a rational government agency would design such an oath even if it would pass constitutional muster.

This discussion should not leave the impression that government agencies have no proper concern with security. The courts have, on the contrary, acknowledged this interest in every case involving loyalty and security issues.[27] But courts have insisted that subversion must be curbed by means that are narrower and more precise than loyalty oaths; indeed, there is reason to believe that people truly bent on sabotage would have few qualms about signing such an oath, while a person of impeccable loyalty but strong conscience might be troubled and would thus forfeit the job for reasons unrelated to any governmental interest. In this way loyalty oaths may actually have been counterproductive, and not simply ineffective or offensive.

May an applicant be asked to list organizations to which he or she belongs? *

The answer depends very much on the scope and purpose of the inquiry. Some years ago, the Supreme Court held that Arkansas could not require all teachers to list every year all the organizations to which they belonged. Such a demand, said the Court, went "far beyond what might be justified in the exercise of the State's legitimate inquiry into the fitness and competency of its teachers" and threatened to deter teachers from perfectly lawful associations.[28] The Court hinted that *some* teachers might be asked at *some* times about *some* associations, but it has had no occasion to define the scope of permissible inquiry in this sensitive area. There may be a difference between requests for information from an initial applicant for public employment and from an incumbent during the term of employment; the Arkansas case was concerned only with the rights of people already employed in the state school system.

The type of organization may also be relevant. It seems

* See footnote to preceding question.

doubtful that government has a valid interest in asking about memberships that would not jeopardize a person's eligibility for employment—that is, groups in which even knowing, active membership would not be disqualifying. Presumably, government has a valid interest only in knowing whether an applicant belongs to an organization that could be outlawed, since other affiliations are protected by the Constitution.

May a police officer be denied employment or fired on the basis of membership in a political party?

In most instances, the answer is probably no, although the issue may have been clouded somewhat by the recent decision of *Foley* v. *Connelie*.[29]

In the past, jobs not protected by civil service were subject to the spoils system under which political connections outweighed merit and seniority as job qualifications. Thus, when a new political party came to power, members of the then-defeated party were subject to dismissal. But the Supreme Court's decision in *Elrod* v. *Burns* put an end to firings of "nonpolicymaking, nonconfidential government" employees who have "satisfactorily perform[ed]" their duties where the dismissals were based "upon the sole ground of . . . political beliefs."[30] Presumably after *Elrod,* non-civil-service law-enforcement officers who are not in confidential policymaking roles could not be fired for being registered Republicans while the Democrats were in power. One's status as a "policymaker" was determined by asking "whether the employee acts as an adviser or formulates plans for the implementation of broad goals."[31]

The Supreme Court decision in *Branti* v. *Finkel* went even further than *Elrod* in protecting public employees from political dismissal.[32] *Branti* involved the dismissal by a newly appointed Democratic public defender of two Republican attorneys in his Rockland County, New York, office. The Supreme Court invalidated the dismissals on the theory that the Constitution protects public employees from political dismissal unless "the hiring authority can demonstrate that party affiliation is an appropriate requirement for the effective performance of the public office involved."[33]

Foley casts some doubt on the application of *Elrod* and *Branti* to police officers, because the majority opinion in

Foley seemingly treated the ordinary state trooper as a high policy-executing official.[34] Taken to its logical extreme, police officers not protected by civil service could be dismissed for membership in the wrong party. Such an outcome is not a likely prospect, however. It is doubtful that the Supreme Court's language in *Foley*, an equal-protection case, would be applied mechanically to the First Amendment context. Indeed, while *Foley* stressed the close connection between the police and the state, it did not suggest that law enforcement should be partisan. Thus, party affiliation poses little danger of job insecurity for the average police officer.

May restrictions be imposed on the political activity of police officers?

Yes. One source of such restrictions may be found in the rules and regulations of individual police departments. For example, the New York City Police Department proscribes police officers from "campaigning for candidates for public office or being a member of a political club" and from "being a candidate for election or serving as a member of a School Board if the School District is located within the City of New York." [35]

A second source, in the case of federal law-enforcement officers such as FBI agents, is the Hatch Act, which restricts the participation in partisan electoral activity of federal employees. The Hatch Act forbids a federal employee from using "his official authority or influence for the purpose of interfering with or affecting the result of an election: or [from taking] an active part in political management or in political campaigns." [36]

A third source of restraint on the political activity of law-enforcement personnel, which applies to state and local police officers, consists of state and local laws modeled after the Hatch Act, so-called "little Hatch Acts." As in the case of the federal law, these state and local statutes restrict the partisan activity of police officers.

An extensive description of the scope and procedures of the Hatch Act and of state and local analogues, including their restrictions on constitutional rights, can be found in Robert O'Neil's *The Rights of Government Employees* on pages 74–84.

May a belief in God be required of police officers?

No. The First Amendment to the Constitution protects all persons against government infringement of the free exercise of religion. The free-exercise clause, however, has never been interpreted to allow the unrestrained practice of religious acts that conflict with vital governmental interests. For example, the Supreme Court recently noted that "courts have sustained government prohibitions on handling venomous snakes or drinking poison, even as part of a religious ceremony." [37] However, the Supreme Court has recognized that the free-exercise clause *absolutely* prohibits "infringements on the 'freedom to believe.' " [38] The freedom to believe, of course, includes the freedom not to believe. Thus, the Court has reaffirmed its earlier decision striking down Maryland's requirement "as a qualification for any office of profit or trust [of] a declaration of belief in the existence of God." [39] Moreover, in *McDaniel* v. *Paty,* the Supreme Court recently invalidated a Tennessee law which barred the clergy from serving in the state legislature.[40]

In short, while practices that pose substantial societal risks may be properly constrained by governmental action, people cannot be forced to espouse any set of religious beliefs. Accordingly, a police officer could not be required to affirm a belief in God, let alone adherence to any particular religion, as a condition of employment. And following *McDaniel* v. *Paty,* the clergy could probably not be barred from serving on a police force, provided of course that their religious beliefs did not impede them from carrying out their duties. The result would likely be different, however, if the cleric's religious beliefs prevented the use of appropriate levels of force, including deadly force, where the circumstances required it.

May a police officer be a member of a sect?

Yes, in most instances.

Certainly a police officer could not be denied employment for his adherence to one of the established religious groups in America. This protection would probably extend to membership in various sects such as Hare Krishna, Children of God, or the Unification Church of Reverend Moon, unless the police department could show that the particular group pursued unlawful ends and that a police officer's membership in that group constituted specific intent to advance the unlawful ends. Of course, members of various sects would still have to perform the duties of a police officer competently.

However, somewhat ironically, current Supreme Court doctrine suggests that a member of Hare Krishna might be allowed to wear his hair in a ponytail or to wear the traditional marking on his forehead, even though, for example, an Irish Catholic police officer could be made subject to the hair-length standards approved by the Court in *Kelley* v. *Johnson*. The reason for this potentially anomalous result is that when First Amendment rights are infringed by governmental action, the government must justify the infringement by showing that substantial governmental interests are served by it.[41] In *Kelley* v. *Johnson*, on the other hand, because First Amendment rights were not at stake and because the Court minimized the privacy interest asserted by the complaining police officer, the police department was required to show merely that its regulations were rationally related to a legitimate governmental objective. There the Court pointed to the department's interest in identifiability and esprit de corps. For the Court to conclude that a Hare Krishna member could be forced to choose between his religion-mandated appearance and his job as a police officer, it would have to raise the interest in identifiability and esprit de corps to the level of substantial interest. Moreover, the department would have to show a clearer relationship between a police department's regulation against ponytails or forehead markings and the advancement of those interests than the minimum rationality permitted in *Kelley* v. *Johnson*. One court recently held that the Navy could prevent a sailor from wearing a religiously required turban because of the Navy's important interest in safety.[42] The court found that safety was impaired because the sailor could not wear a helmet and because naval activities are conducted in close proximity to complex machinery of an often hazardous nature. It is questionable, however, whether a mark on the forehead or a short ponytail implicates a police department's interest in safety to the same extent. Obviously, a religious practice that impairs safety or efficiency, such as wearing flowing robes, must yield to those interests.

May a police officer be denied employment if his religious beliefs prevent him from working at certain times?

Yes, provided that the department has attempted reasonably to accommodate the individual's needs and that further accommodation would cause undue hardship to the department.

In *United States* v. *City of Albuquerque,* a case brought under Title VII of the Civil Rights Act of 1964 and not the First Amendment, a Seventh-Day Adventist was fired from his job as a firefighter for refusing to report to work on a particular Saturday since to do so would have conflicted with his religious beliefs.[43] The firefighter contended that his dismissal constituted unlawful religious discrimination in violation of Title VII which, among other things, prohibits discrimination in employment on the basis of religion. The Court upheld his dismissal for two reasons: (1) the City of Albuquerque had attempted to make "reasonable accommodations" to the firefighter's religious practices by following a "fairly liberal time off policy" and by allowing vacation leaves, leaves without pay, and swapping shifts; and (2) the firefighter had been "intransigent" in his refusal to " 'work it out' within the existing rules of the department." [44] Thus, the department had attempted reasonably to accommodate the employee's needs, and further accommodation would cause undue hardship to the city, since when the "employer is protecting the lives and property of a dependent citizenry, courts should go slow in restructuring his employment practices." [45]

Similar considerations would apply to police officers alleging that they are victims of religious discrimination. The hardship allowed to be imposed on police and fire departments is evidently less than on private employers because police officers and firefighters must protect life and property. Still, it is important to note that "to a very great degree each case turns on its own particular facts and circumstances." [46]

The Equal Employment Opportunity Commission recently promulgated regulations interpreting the prohibition against religious discrimination in Title VII of the Civil Rights Act. The regulations require an employer to make reasonable accommodations to the religious practices of its employees. Employers are advised to investigate flexible scheduling, lateral transfer and change of job assignments, and voluntary substitutes through swapping as possible means of accommodation. An employer may refuse to accommodate the employee if it can prove that it would suffer undue hardship. Undue hardship does not include the infrequent payment of premium wages for a substitute; nor does it include the payment of administrative costs incurred in providing the accommodation. The regulations also define very broadly a protected "religious practice . . . to include moral or ethical beliefs as to what is right and wrong which are sincerely held with the strength of traditional religious views." [47]

May a police officer practice his or her religion on duty?
Only in very limited ways.

Even though an off-duty officer may worship publicly,[48] may distribute religious literature,[49] may proselytize,[50] and may not be denied employment on the basis of religion, an officer may not use his or her position as a pulpit. The First Amendment protects the free exercise of religion, but it also prohibits the establishment of a state religion, as well as excessive entanglements between church and state. In *McDaniel* v. *Paty,* the Supreme Court ruled that Tennessee could not force a person to choose between political and religious expression. But if a police department simply forbade on-duty proselytizing, its restriction would be supported by the First Amendment's nonestablishment provision and by the needs of discipline and esprit de corps. On the other hand, if an officer chose to study religious texts during lunch hour, or to recite a prayer at his or her desk at various points during the day, or to obey religious dietary laws during breaks and meals, a department would have a harder time justifying a prohibition, unless the religious practice was disruptive of the force.

May police officers criticize departmental policy?
The answer is a qualified yes. Disciplinary action may be taken against a police officer if there is a specific finding that the officer's exercise of his free-speech rights impaired his efficiency as a police officer or the police department's effectiveness in fulfilling its responsibilities.[51]

In a case decided several years ago by the United States

Court of Appeals for the District of Columbia, *Tygrett* v. *Washington,* the court held unlawful a probationary police officer's dismissal for his public advocacy in the Washington, D.C., newspapers of a "sick-out" in the event police officers were not granted a pay raise.[52] The court first noted that the sole cause of the officer's dismissal was his public call for an epidemic of "Blue flu." Since there was no possibility that he had been fired for alternative independent reasons that were legally adequate, the First Amendment issue was thus squarely presented.[53] Utilizing the Supreme Court's balancing approach of *Pickering* v. *Board of Education,* the Court of Appeals noted that ordinarily a court must weigh the police officer's free-speech rights against the police department's interest in efficiently carrying out its public responsibilities.[54] But because the district court had never specifically determined that the officer's free-speech activities actually imperiled the police department's efficiency, an essential showing whose burden rests on the department and not the officer, the court did not have to balance the respective interests.

In another case, *Brukiewa* v. *Police Commissioner,* the Maryland Court of Appeals reached a similar result.[55] In that case, a Baltimore police officer appeared on a local television station. During the broadcast, he strongly criticized departmental morale. The officer was subsequently disciplined. However, the Maryland Court of Appeals upheld the officer's free-speech rights. The court noted that the officer's

> personal fitness to perform his daily police duties . . . was not impaired. . . . His statements were not directed towards a superior with whom he would come into daily or frequent contact. . . . His statements were not charged, shown or found to have affected discipline or harmony or the general efficiency or effectiveness of the police department.[56]

In practice, what must a police department show to justify disciplinary action?

If the department can show that a police officer's public enunciation of his opinions impaired either the officer's competence to do his job or the department's ability to fulfill its public duty, the officer can be disciplined. To meet this burden, "there must be a clear and direct relationship . . . between the articulated grounds for an adverse personnel action" and the harm to the employee's or the employer's effective functioning.[57] Moreover, even if the officer can show that a constitutionally impermissible factor figured in the department's decision, the employer can still justify its actions if it demonstrates "by a preponderance of the evidence that it would have reached the same decision . . . even in the absence of the protected conduct." [58] As the Supreme Court reasoned in *Mount Healthy City Board of Education* v. *Doyle,* a government employee "ought not to be able, by engaging in [constitutionally protected] conduct, to prevent his employer from assessing his performance record" and responding appropriately.[59] In other words, disciplinary action supported by constitutionally adequate grounds does not become invalid because impermissible reasons also contributed to the decision.

A police department's ability to meet its burden of proof will depend on many factors, including the time and place of the statements, as well as the officer's influence on the force and the volatility of the context in which the comments are made. To illustrate, the case of *Phillips* v. *Adult Probation Department* [60] involved a deputy probation officer whose work included enforcement of divorce settlements and child-support agreements. In September 1970 the plaintiff hung on his office wall a poster sympathetic to Angela Davis, H. Rap Brown, and Eldridge Cleaver, all of whom were fugitives from the FBI at the time.[61] In upholding his disciplining by the agency, the Ninth Circuit Court of Appeals considered several factors: the contemporary political climate, the timing and location of his political statement (on-duty, in the office), and the inappropriateness of glorifying lawbreakers in a law-enforcement agency. The court distinguished an earlier case, *Waters* v. *Peterson,*[62] which had upheld several government employees' right to demonstrate against two supervisors' alleged racial prejudice. The crucial difference between the cases was that *Waters* involved gathering and sign-carrying during lunch hour (off-duty) in a public cafeteria (nonofficial), and the employees' message did not implicitly contradict the agency's policies, as Phillips's poster did.

As a practical matter, it would seem relatively easy for the police department to meet its burden of showing impaired efficiency where a police officer has advocated, for example, a sick-out by fellow employees, especially if his or her statements are made in a volatile context when a sick-out might occur. On the other hand, it would be much more difficult to prove impaired efficiency if an off-duty officer publicly criticized a department policy that entailed, for example, the arrest of prostitutes. Criticizing such a policy and articulating the view that victimless crimes should not siphon off police resources would, in most conceivable contexts, be protected free speech. It would be difficult for the department to show that such a public position hindered the officer's or the department's functioning.

But it is not impossible. In *Byrd* v. *Gain*, for example, the Ninth Circuit refused to expunge reprimands from the records of two officers who had issued a press release and had made public statements criticizing the San Francisco department's stop-and-frisk policy, which the officers claimed to have an unfair impact on black males.[63] The court would not protect employees who had "publicly . . . hector[ed] their department and its superior officers by language calculated to inflame the public . . . against the police and to affect adversely the morale and discipline of the department." [64]

One further warning: Even if an officer may publicly espouse a viewpoint without fear of reprisal (for instance, the criticism of expending resources on victimless crimes), the officer is not protected against discipline if he or she refuses to implement the policy while on duty.

May a police officer criticize co-workers or superiors?
That depends upon the nature of the criticism.

Most police-department regulations establish internal procedures for handling complaints against co-workers or superiors on grounds, for example, of incompetence or corruption. But suppose a police officer is dissatisfied with the results of internal procedures and airs his or her criticisms publicly. Would it offend the First Amendment if the officer were fired? The *Pickering* case indicates that the speech rights of an officer may be curtailed when criticism of a superior (or of a co-worker) demonstrably upsets the harmonious working relationship needed for a smoothly functioning police department.[65]

Suppose instead that, after exhausting internal procedures, a police officer remains dissatisfied and reasonably claims in a radio broadcast that a co-worker or superior took bribes from organized-crime figures or drug pushers. A public allegation of such illegal activity would undoubtedly disrupt the working relationship between the accusing and the accused officers. But the accusing officer would almost certainly be protected from reprisal provided he or she first gave the department itself an opportunity to clean its own house before going public.

Many police departments, as part of their internal regulations, prevent vindictive actions against police officers who charge their fellow officers with illegal activity. In the case of the FBI, an accusing agent is given explicit statutory protection against vindictive personnel action when the agent informs the Attorney General of information which he "reasonably believes evidences (i) a violation of any law, rule, or regulation, or (ii) mismanagement, a gross waste of funds, an abuse of authority, or a substantial and specific danger to public health or safety." [66] While an officer or an FBI agent could probably be disciplined for not following the rule of first complaining internally before going public, the First Amendment would probably prevent disciplinary action if the officer or agent made public accusations after following internal procedures.

In the absence of such regulatory or statutory procedures and protections, the Constitution may protect accusing officers, at least where the public charge is one of illegality. The governmental interest in preserving harmonious working relationships among officers is weakened when the activity complained of involves illegality. Certainly, the government has no legitimate interest in preventing the disclosure of illegality. Since the government has no substantial interest to balance against the free-speech rights of the accusing officer, it would likely be unconstitutional to impair those First Amendment rights by taking punitive action against the accusing officer.

Is a police officer entitled to a warning about the type of criticism that is forbidden?

There is no clear answer, since the courts are divided.

One court has by implication assumed that the constitutional doctrine of "void for vagueness," which has developed principally in the area of criminal law, applies to the free-speech rights of police officers.[67] The doctrine protects individuals from being punished pursuant to a statute or regulation if the average person would have difficulty in understanding what behavior was prohibited. In a case before the Ninth Circuit Court of Appeals, a police officer challenged as unconstitutionally vague a departmental regulation prohibiting " 'unofficerlike conduct' which 'tends to subvert the good order, efficiency or discipline of [the] Department.' " Although the court upheld the disciplining of a police lieutenant for making disparaging remarks about a superior while addressing subordinates during morning inspection, the court did recognize that the same regulation might "be susceptible to vagueness challenges in some contexts." [68] The court suggested that if in a particular context there was a reasonable doubt about whether certain types of remarks might undermine departmental order, efficiency and discipline, then the regulation might be unconstitutionally vague as applied in that context. Subsequently, the Ninth Circuit upheld a San Francisco Police Department rule that authorized punishment for conduct that "reflects discredit" upon the department.[69] Two police officers had made statements to the press accusing the Department of racial harassment of minority citizens. The court upheld the rule both on its face and as applied in the specific context. The earlier suggestion by the same court that such a rule might be unconstitutional in some instances is now doubtful, at least in the Ninth Circuit.

Closely related to the vagueness doctrine is the overbreadth doctrine. This will serve to invalidate a police department regulation that is overbroad—so broad that while it proscribes activity that the department may legitimately regulate, it also sweeps "constitutionally protected activity within its ambit." [70] In *Gasparinetti* v. *Kerr,* the Third Circuit Court of Appeals held a number of regulations of the Newark Police Department unconstitutionally overbroad.[71] For example, the court invalidated regulations proscribing (1) "derogatory reference to Department orders or instructions," (2) "censure [of] other Department members concerning official transactions," and (3) statements that "publicly disparage or comment unfavorably or disrespectfully on the official action of a superior officer." [72]

The practical impact of the decision will be to require police departments to write narrow regulations when they attempt to control police officers' speech. If the regulation is so broad that it would also prohibit constitutionally protected activity, it will be invalidated.[73]

May a police department require officers to sign "secrecy" agreements with respect to post-termination publications?

Perhaps.

In the recent case of *Snepp* v. *United States,* the Supreme Court upheld an employment agreement between Snepp, a CIA agent, and the CIA.[74] In the agreement, Snepp promised not to disclose classified information without CIA authorization and not to publish any information or material relating to the CIA without prior CIA approval. Snepp violated his agreement when he wrote and published without CIA clearance *Decent Interval,* concerning CIA activities in South Vietnam. Even though the Government acknowledged that no classified information was published, the Supreme Court agreed that breach of the promise not to submit the manuscript for prior CIA approval required a special remedy: all of the profits from the book were to be turned over to the Government.

This extraordinary decision by the Supreme Court potentially allows a local police department or federal law-enforcement agency to require their officers to enter similar secrecy agreements. Hopefully, in such cases the Supreme Court would limit such prior restraints to the national-security context, even though the *Snepp* decision did not in so many words rely on a national security rationale.

NOTES

1. MASS. GEN. LAWS ANN., ch 264, §14 (West) *quoted in* Cole v. Richardson, 405 U.S. 676, 678 n. 1 (1972).
2. R. O'NEIL, THE RIGHTS OF GOVERNMENT EMPLOYEES 49 (1978).

3. Baggett v. Bullitt, 377 U.S. 360, 362 (1964).

4. Elfbrandt v. Russell, 384 U.S. 11, 17 (1966).

5. 425 U.S. 238 (1978).

6. *See* Kelley v. Johnson, 425 U.S. at 245–46, indicating that police officers of Suffolk County must salute the flag while in uniform. This provision was not challenged and the Court seemed to assume its validity.

7. In West Virginia State Bd. of Educ. v. Barnette, 319 U.S. 624 (1942), the Supreme Court struck down a requirement that school pupils salute the flag of the United States while reciting the pledge of allegiance. The Court found that the flag-salute rule amounted to "a compulsion of students to declare a belief." *Id.* at 631.

8. *See* Slocum v. Fire and Police Commission of East Peoria, 8 Ill. App. 3d 465, 290 N.E.2d 28 (1972).

9. 430 U.S. 705 (1977).

10. Blameuser v. Andrews, 49 U.S.L.W. 2225 (7th Cir. Sept. 22, 1980) (self-proclaimed membership in Nazi party and public espousal of its beliefs held demonstrably incompatible with duties of military officer); *see* Note, *The Policeman: Must He Be a Second-Class Citizen with Regard to His First Amendment Rights?* 46 N.Y.U.L. Rev. 536, 546 (1971).

11. 5. U.S.C. §2903 (1976); *compare* United Fed'n of Postal Clerks v. Blount, 325 F. Supp. 879 (D.D.C.), *aff'd*, 404 U.S. 802 (1971) (upholding constitutionality), *with* Stewart v. Washington, 301 F. Supp. 610 (D.D.C. 1969) (held unconstitutional). FBI agents are classified within the excepted service, as opposed to the competitive service, of the Civil Service. *See* 5 U.S.C. §§2102 (a)(1)(A) & 7103 (a)(3)(B).

12. 5. U.S.C. §3331 (loyalty oath); 5 U.S.C. §7311 (affidavit).

13. *See* Police Officers' Guild v. Washington, 369 F. Supp. 543 (D.D.C. 1973) (three-judge court).

14. 5 U.S.C. §7532.

15. Cole v. Young, 351 U.S. 536, 541–42, 551 (1956).

16. *Id.; see* Leiner v. United States, 181 F. Supp. 400 (Ct. Cl. 1958) (postal employee not in "sensitive" position).

17. Exec. Order No. 11,905, 41 Fed. Reg. 7703 (1976) *superseded by* Exec. Order No. 12,036, 43 Fed Reg. 3674 (1978), *reprinted in* 50 U.S.C. §401 (notes following statute).

18. Exec. Order No. 12,036, *supra* note 17.

90   THE RIGHTS OF POLICE OFFICERS

19. 5 U.S.C. §7532(a)(c).
20. 5 U.S.C. §7532(b).
21. Exec. Order No. 10,450, §8(a), 18 Fed. Reg. 2489 (1953), as amended, *reprinted following* 5 U.S.C. §7311 (1976 and Supp. 1978).
22. *Id.* §7; 5 U.S.C. §§3571, 7312.
23. Bruns v. Pomerlau, 319 F. Supp. 58 (D. Md. 1970).
24. Cramp v. Board of Pub. Instruction, 368 U.S. 278 (1961).
25. Keyishian v. Board of Regents, 385 U.S. 589 (1967).
26. United States v. Brown, 381 U.S. 437 (1965).
27. Baggett v. Bullitt, 377 U.S. 360, 379–80 (1964).
28. Shelton v. Tucker, 364 U.S. 479 (1960).
29. 435 U.S. 291 (1978).
30. 427 U.S. 347, 375 (1976) (Stewart, J., concurring).
31. *Id.* at 368.
32. Branti v. Finkel, 48 U.S.L.W. 4331 (U.S. Apr. 1, 1980).
33. *Id.*
34. *See* 435 U.S. at 310 (Stevens, J., dissenting).
35. New York City Police Department Patrol Guide (General Regulations) at 2 (1978). *See also* Kelley v. Johnson, 425 U.S. 238, 246 (1976).
36. 5 U.S.C. §7324(a).
37. McDaniel v. Paty, 435 U.S. 618, 628 n. 8 (1978), *citing* State *ex rel.* Swann v. Pack, 527 S.W. 2d 99 (Tenn. 1975), *cert. denied,* 424 U.S. 954 (1976).
38. *Id.* at 627, 634 (Brennan, J., concurring in the judgment.)
39. Torcaso v. Watkins, 367 U.S. 488 (1961).
40. 435 U.S. at 621.
41. *See* Sherwood v. Brown, 619 F.2d 47 (9th Cir. 1980), *cert. denied,* 49 U.S.L.W. 3289 (U.S. Oct. 20, 1980) (No. 80–218) (U.S. Navy's interest in safety held sufficient to outweigh First Amendment interest in wearing religiously required turban).
42. *Id.*
43. 545 F.2d 110 (10th Cir. 1976), *cert. denied,* 433 U.S. 909 (1977).
44. *Id.* at 113.
45. *Id.* at 114.
46. *Id.* at 115.
47. *See* 45 Fed. Reg. No. 213, at 72610–15 (Oct. 31, 1980).
48. Kunz v. New York, 340 U.S. 290 (1951).
49. Murdock v. Pennsylvania, 319 U.S. 105 (1943).

50. United Pub. Workers v. Mitchell, 331 U.S. 75, 100 (1947) (dictum).

51. *See* Pickering v. Board of Educ., 391 U.S. 563, 568 (1968).

52. 534 F.2d 840 (D.C. Cir. 1974).

53. *Id.* at 845; *cf.* Mount Healthy City Bd. of Educ. v. Doyle, 429 U.S. 274 (1977).

54. *Id.*

55. 257 Md. 36 (1970).

56. *Id.* at 52.

57. Doe v. Hampton, 566 F.2d 265, 272 (D.C. Cir. 1977).

58. 429 U.S. at 287.

59. *Id.* at 286.

60. 491 F.2d 951 (9th Cir. 1974); *accord,* Goldenwasser v. Brown, 417 F.2d 1169 (D.C. Cir. 1969), *cert. denied,* 397 U.S. 922 (1970).

61. 491 F.2d at 952.

62. 496 F2d 91 (D.C. Cir. 1973).

63. 558 F.2d 553 (9th Cir. 1977), *cert. denied,* 434 U.S. 1087 (1978).

64. *Id.* at 554.

65. 543 F.2d at 570; *see* Kannisto v. City and County of San Francisco, 541 F.2d 841, 844 (9th Cir. 1976), *cert. denied,* 430 U.S. 931 (1977); Fuentes v. Roher, 519 F.2d 379 (2d Cir. 1975).

66. 5 U.S.C. §2303(b)(8)(B) (Supp. II 1978).

67. Kannisto v. City and County of San Francisco, 541 F.2d 841, 844 (9th Cir. 1976), *cert. denied,* 430 U.S. 931 (1977).

68. *Id.*

69. Byrd v. Gain, 558 F.2d 553 (9th Cir. 1977), *cert. denied,* 434 U.S. 1087 (1978).

70. Grayned v. City of Rockford, 408 U.S. 104, 114 (1972).

71. 568 F.2d 311 (3d Cir. 1977), *cert. denied,* 436 U.S. 903, (1978).

72. *Id.* at 314.

73. *See* Flynn v. Giarrusso, 321 F. Supp. 1295 (E.D. La. 1971) (court invalidated a police department regulation which provided that a "member shall not unjustly criticize or ridicule, or express hatred or contempt toward, or indulge in remarks which may be detrimental to . . . any person").

74. Snepp v. United States, 48 U.S.L.W. 3527 (U.S. Feb. 19, 1980).

IV

Labor Law: Unions, Collective Bargaining, and Work Stoppages

The labor rights of police officers differ substantially from those of nongovernment workers, and even from those of government employees whose work is not related to public safety. The labor rights of the typical working person are secured in part by the National Labor Relations Act (NLRA).[1] The bundle of rights protected by the NLRA, however, most significantly the rights to bargain collectively and to strike,[2] does not extend to any government employees, including police officers.[3] Nor does the Landrum-Griffin Act—which, among other things, secures to covered employees certain rights directed at ensuring democratic governance of unions and protecting free-speech rights of union members—extend to police officers.[4] Furthermore, federal courts have suggested that police officers may be entitled to less constitutional protection in their labor-related associational rights than are other government employees, such as librarians for example.[5]

This chapter deals primarily with the protection afforded by the First Amendment to labor-related associational rights, with collective-bargaining and strike rights under state law and the Constitution, and with rights related to the police officer's status vis-à-vis his or her union and the union's status vis-à-vis the employer. Chapter III should be consulted for a fuller discussion of First Amendment rights generally. Chapter IX, Section C, treats questions of unnecessarily dangerous working conditions and their relationship to collective bargaining.

Could Congress, if it were so inclined, extend the NLRA's rights to bargain collectively and to strike to police officers?

The answer is unclear.

The 1976 case of *National League of Cities* v. *Usery* limited Congress's commerce-clause power where its exercise impinged on essential governmental functions of the state.[6] In that case, the Supreme Court struck down the application of congressional minimum-wage and hour standards to state employees on the theory that the Tenth Amendment—which "reserve[s] to the States respectively, or to the people" those "powers not delegated to the United States by the Constitution, nor prohibited by it to the States"—limited Congress's expansive commerce-clause power. Arguably, a grant by Congress of collective-bargaining and strike rights to police officers would be more intrusive of essential state governmental functions than was the legislation struck down in *National League of Cities*. On the other hand, Congress might extend such rights pursuant to its authority to enforce the Fourteenth Amendment and the rights applicable against the states through the Fourteenth Amendment.

What is the source of police officers' labor rights?

The First Amendment protects the rights of police officers to free association. Accordingly, police officers have a constitutionally protected right to form and to join a labor union.[7] Police officers may even join unions that advocate illegal activity, such as illegal strikes by police officers, provided the officer does not act illegally.[8] Government officials faced with possible illegal activity must tailor their responses to eliminate the illegality only, without unnecessarily infringing on the constitutional rights of police officers. The balancing of first amendment rights against governmental interests was discussed in Chapter III.

A second source of protection for the labor rights of police officers is state law. Clearly, the level of protection will vary from one state to another, although it can never be less than what is secured by the First Amendment. However, because the First Amendment and the NLRA do not encompass the right to compel a governmental employer to bargain collectively, police officers must look to state law as the source of their collective-bargaining rights.[9] For example, the Commonwealth of Massachusetts does not exclude police officers from those public employees who have

> the right of self-organization and the right to form, join, or assist any employee organization for the purpose of bargaining collectively through representatives of their own choosing on questions of wages, hours, and other terms and conditions of employment, and to engage in lawful, concerted activities for the purpose of collective bargaining or other mutual aid or protection, free from interference, restraint, or coercion.[10]

Accordingly, the full range of labor rights applies to police officers in Massachusetts to the same extent that it applies to other public employees.[11] Still, even Massachusetts law says, "No public employee or employee organization shall engage in a strike, and no public employee or employee organization shall induce, encourage or condone any strike, work stoppage, slowdown or withholding of services by such public employees."[12] Thus, strikes, which might otherwise be permissible in the private sector, are illegal when undertaken by police officers in Massachusetts and most other jurisdictions.

Do police officers have a right to join a labor union?
As noted above, police officers have a constitutional right to join a labor union. Moreover, that right extends to membership in a labor union which " 'holds, claims or uses' the right to strike," provided the officer does not actually strike if it is prohibited by applicable law.[13] In *Police Officers' Guild* v. *Washington,* the plaintiff union challenged a District of Columbia law which prohibited "police officers, under pain of immediate discharge, from associating freely and from becoming members of or affiliating with any organization which 'holds, claims or uses' the right to strike."[14] The three-judge court held that the statute was "so overbroad as to unconstitutionally impinge plaintiffs' right to freedom of association protected under the First Amendment."[15] The court noted that the "unique and special nature of a policeman's obligation to serve the public justifies state control and prohibition of

some activities in which he would otherwise be free to engage," but concluded that the challenged statute prohibited both legal and illegal activity.[16] The constitutionally protected activity which was proscribed by the statute included, among other things, the right to advocate, to assert, or simply to entertain "thoughts of achieving the right to strike against the District of Columbia Government," as well as the right to join a union which was affiliated with another union that advocated the right to strike.[17] Thus, the court concluded that while the government may adopt legislation which is precisely crafted to protect the public interest in preventing strikes by police officers, the broad proscription at issue in *Washington* did not do the job.

Can supervisors or administrators be barred from unions to which rank-and-file police officers belong?

Yes.

Robert O'Neil writes in *The Rights of Government Employees* that there is disagreement among courts about whether supervisory government personnel and rank-and-file employees may belong to the same union. A federal district court in Florida, for example, upheld the First Amendment rights of supervisors and classroom teachers to associate in the same union.[18] However, the result is likely to be different in the case of police officers, where the governmental interests in discipline and in avoiding conflicts of interest between supervisors and rank-and-file officers may outweigh the First Amendment interest in free association. *Elk Grove Firefighters* v. *Willis* held that captains and lieutenants of the local fire department could be prevented from associating in the same union as rank-and-file firefighters in order to preserve discipline and to avoid conflicts of interest.[19] A similar result would be likely in the case of police officers.

Do police officers have a right to bargain collectively?

No, unless it is available under state or local law. There is no constitutional right to mandatory collective bargaining.[20] Accordingly, a state or local governmental entity cannot be required, as a matter of federal constitutional law, to bargain collectively with the police officers' union.[21] Nevertheless, a state or local government may provide for such collective bargaining. Approximately three quarters of the states provide for collective bargaining with specified public employees.[22] However, these states do not necessarily extend collective-bargaining protection to police officers. For example. Missouri excludes officers (and teachers) from collective bargaining even though other public employees have that right; on the other hand, Massachusetts, New York, and Michigan, for example, recognize the collective-bargaining rights of police officers.[23]

The distinction drawn between the rights of certain government employees and the rights of personnel responsible for public safety was challenged on constitutional grounds in *Confederation of Police* v. *City of Chicago*. The federal district court held that it was constitutionally permissible to accord police officers less labor-related protection than that accorded to other governmental employees.

Do police officers have a constitutional right to a departmental grievance procedure?

No, except where state law has created an applicable property right. Before police officers can claim a procedural right under the Constitution, they must establish that the department's action has deprived them of "liberty" or "property" within the meaning of the due-process clause of the Fourteenth Amendment. In *Confederation of Police* v. *City of Chicago*, the U.S. Court of Appeals for the Seventh Circuit, relying on Supreme Court doctrine, held that due process is required when state law creates an "expectation that a particular employment relationship will continue unless certain defined events occur." [24] (This subject is considered in greater detail in Chapter VII). Of course, state law may provide for such a procedure, as South Carolina does, even though the state is not under a constitutional obligation to do so, or it may be established as part of a collective-bargaining agreement.

Do police officers have a constitutional right to strike or to conduct work slow-downs?

No. Police officers, whether union members or not, do not have a federal constitutional right to strike or to conduct work slowdowns.[25] Accordingly, a state may forbid

strikes, sick-ins, and related activities, consistent with constitutional requirements. As part of the prohibition, a state
may punish police officers who violate a valid state law.
For example, individuals may be held in contempt of
court if they disobey an order to return to work. In addition, state law, such as New York's Taylor Law, may
authorize fines for illegal work stoppages; and dismissal,
loss of pay, and, in the case of the District of Columbia
and the State of Nebraska, imprisonment are also statu-
torily authorized sanctions for such activity.[26]

Do police-officer unions owe a duty of fair representa-
tion to union members?

Yes. The duty of fair representation owed by unions to
union members has been delineated with greater elabora-
tion in the private sector than in the public sector, but
there is clearly an evolving duty of fair representation imposed upon public-employee unions.[27] In general terms,
the duty of fair representation flows from a union's "status
as exclusive bargaining representative." Accordingly,
courts have held that such unions must "represent fairly
all employees in the bargaining unit." This general requirement has been extended to forbid unions from engaging
in "any form of discrimination or unfair treatment of any
employees in the bargaining unit. It encompasses the
negotiation of the collective bargaining agreement, the
processing of a grievance, including the decision whether
to press a grievance to arbitration, and the presentation
of the grievance in arbitration." [28]

Breaches of the duty of fair representation range in
scope from racial discrimination by a union to the failure
by a union to follow timeliness requirements imposed by
the collective-bargaining agreement. Thus, where a union
negotiates different benefits for its black members than for
its white members [29] or where a union fails "to name its
arbitrator within the contractual time limits (5 days) [and
thereby] renders the grievance non-arbitrable," [30] the courts
have found breaches of the duty of fair representation.
Similarly, a union violated its duty of fair representation
when it sided with one union member rather than another
without investigating the relative qualifications of the two
members when both sought the same promotion.[31] The
common denominator of the various cases is that unions

must act in good faith in a manner that is neither discriminatory nor arbitrary.[32]

For an extensive discussion of the duty of fair representation in the private sector, including such topics as the specific nature of the union's duty in negotiating a collective bargaining agreement, in processing an individual's grievance, and in taking a grievance to arbitration, see *The Rights of Union Members,* by Clyde W. Summers and Robert J. Rabin, pages 117–36 Avon Books, 1979. While their discussion treats the private sector almost exclusively, the analogous duty of fair representation in the public sector makes much of their discussion relevant.

May a police officer refuse to join a union?

Yes, but the officer can nevertheless be required to pay dues to the union that has been recognized as the exclusive bargaining agent for the unit where he or she works. "Even a conscientious desire not to support the union could not relieve the [officer] of an obligation (if imposed under state law) to pay union dues." [33]

In *Abood* v. *Detroit Board of Education,* the Supreme Court was faced with the question whether such a Michigan law violated the constitutional rights of government employees.[34] That law authorized a union and a local government employer "to agree to an 'agency shop' arrangement, whereby every employee represented by a union—even though not a union member—must pay to the union, as a condition of employment, a service fee equal in amount to union dues." [35] The agency-shop arrangement challenged by a class of Detroit teachers required all teachers who had not become union members within sixty days of being hired to pay the service charge to the union. The Court noted that compelling employees "to support their collective bargaining representative has an impact upon their First Amendment interests," since an "employee may very well have ideological objections to a wide variety of activities undertaken by the union." [36] The Court upheld the law insofar as it required employees to pay for costs related to collective bargaining. However, where the union spends money on the expression or advancement of ideological views, dues may not be coerced from employees who object to the advancement of such ideology.

While Michigan permits public-sector agency-shop arrangements, most states "prohibit the typical private-sector union-security arrangement" in the case of public employees.[37]

May a police officers' union insist that union dues be withheld from police officers' paychecks?

No. In *City of Charlotte* v. *Firefighters Local 660,*[38] the Supreme Court held against a union of firefighters which challenged the refusal of Charlotte, North Carolina, to withhold union dues, even though the city permitted a checkoff for employee contributions to savings plans, retirement programs, and certain charities.[39] The Court held that the city's distinction between programs of general interest on the one hand and the withholding of union dues on the other hand was rational. Moreover, the Court found no constitutional underpinning for the union's attempt to compel withholding of its members' dues.

NOTES

1. 29 U.S.C. §§151–168 (1976).
2. *Id.* §157.
3. *Id.* §152(2); *see* C. MORRIS, THE DEVELOPING LABOR LAW 209 (1971).
4. C. SUMMERS & R. RABIN, THE RIGHTS OF UNION MEMBERS 24 (1979).
5. *E.g.,* Confederation of Police v. City of Chicago, 382 F. Supp. 624 (N.D. Ill. 1974), *aff'd,* 547 F.2d 375 (7th Cir. 1977). ·
6. 426 U.S. 833 (1976).
7. *See* Police Officers' Guild v. Washington, 369 F. Supp. 543 (D.D.C. 1973) (three-judge court).
8. *Id.* at 553; MASS. GEN. LAWS ANN. ch. 150E, §9A(2) (West Supp. 1979).
9. Confederation of Police v. City of Chicago, 382 F. Supp. 624 (N.D. Ill. 1974), *aff'd,* 547 F.2d 375 (7th Cir. 1977).
10. MASS. GEN. LAWS ANN. ch. 150E, §2 (West Supp. 1979).
11. *See generally* Labor Relations Comm. v. Town of Natick, 369 Mass. 431, 339 N.E.2d 900 (Mass. 1976).
12. MASS. GEN. LAWS ANN. ch. 150E, §9A (West Supp. 1979).
13. *See* Police Officers' Guild v. Washington, 369 F. Supp. at 544.
14. *Id.*

15. *Id.* at 550.
16. *Id.* at 551.
17. *Id.* at 552.
18. Orr v. Thorp, 308 F. Supp. 1369 (S.D. Fla. 1969).
19. 400 F. Supp. 1097 (N.D. Ill. 1975), *aff'd,* 539 F.2d 714 (7th Cir. 1976); R. O'NEIL, THE RIGHTS OF GOVERNMENT EMPLOYEES 92 (1978).
20. Confederation of Police v. City of Chicago, 382 F. Supp. at 628.
21. *See* Atkins v. City of Charlotte, 296 F. Supp. 1068, 1077 (W.D.N.C. 1969).
22. Note, Private Damage Actions Against Public Sector Unions for Illegal Strikes, 91 Harv L. Rev. 1309, 1309 n. 4 (1978).
23. Mo. Ann. Stat. §§105. 500–530 (Vernon Supp. 1978); MASS. GEN. LAWS ANN. ch 150E §2 (West. Supp. 1979); N.Y. CIV. SERV. LAW, art. 14, §§200, 204 (McKinney 1973); MICH. COMP. LAWS §423.209 (1978). State Statutes are collected in Note, *supra* note 22 at 1309–11, nn 49.
24. Confederation of Police v. City of Chicago, 547 F.2d 375, 376 (7th Cir. 1977) (relying on Bishop v. Wood, 426 U.S. 341 (1976)).
25. *See* Lontine v. Van Cleave, 483 F.2d 966 (10th Cir. 1973); Vorbeck v. McNeal, 407 F. Supp. 733 (E.D. Mo. 1976), *aff'd,* 426 U.S. 943 (1976); Police Officers' Guild v. Washington, 369 F. Supp. 543 (D.D.C. 1973).
26. *See* N.Y. CIV. SERV. LAW, art. 14, §210 (McKinney, 1973); Note, *supra* note 22, at 1311 n. 9.
27. SUMMERS & RABIN, *supra* note 4, at 132; Belanger v. Matteson, 346 A.2d 124 (R.I.S.Ct. 1975); *see* Jackson v. Regional Transit Service, 54 App. Div. 2d 305, 388 N.Y.S.2d 441 (4th Dept. 1976).
28. SUMMERS & RABIN, *supra* note 4, at 117–18.
29. *See* Steele v. Louisville Railroad Co., 323 U.S. 192 (1944).
30. Jackson v. Regional Transit Service, 388 N.Y.S.2d at 442.
31. Berlanger v. Matteson, 346 A.2d at 131–32.
32. SUMMERS & RABIN, *supra* note 4, at 118–22.
33. O'NEIL, *supra* note 19, at 91.
34. 431 U.S. 209 (1977).
35. *Id.* at 211.
36. *Id.* at 222.
37. SUMMERS & RABIN, *supra* note 4, at 145.
38. 426 U.S. 283 (1976).
39. O'NEIL, *supra* note 19, at 91.

V

The Private Lives
of Police Officers

Unmarried coupling, "swinging," open homosexuality, nudism on weekends, and sporting sideburns. Their common denominator is the risk suffered by employees who engage in the behavior. Usually the government can regulate the private lives of its police officers only when off-duty conduct adversely affects on-duty performance. This rule is based on the precept that the government must act as a rational employer.[1] But the usual rule is not always invoked, and the outcome often turns on the particular facts involved. Thus, courts have wrestled with issues as diverse as nontraditional sexual relationships and old-fashioned muttonchops. Somewhat surprisingly, the first is often protected from departmental regulation, but the second clearly is not.

The questions in this chapter fall into several categories: sources of protection; heterosexual associations; homosexual associations; other personal associations; grooming and dress codes; and procedural protections. Questions regarding a police officer's right to bear children were treated in Chapter II; questions about the officer's place of residence and drug-related activity, in Chapter I; and questions about the officer's political opinions and associations, in Chapter III.

A. SOURCES OF PROTECTION

What are privacy rights?

In 1928, Justice Brandeis wrote:

the makers of our Constitution undertook to secure conditions favorable to the pursuit of happiness. They recognized the significance of man's spiritual nature, of his feelings and his intellect. They knew that only a part of the pain, pleasure, and satisfaction of life are to be found in material things. They sought to protect Americans in their beliefs, their thoughts, their emotions and their sensations. They conferred, as against the government, the right to be let alone—the most comprehensive of rights and the right most valued by civilized men.[2]

What are the sources of privacy rights?

First and foremost, the U.S. Constitution. Isolating the particular provision is more difficult. Privacy rights have been traced to the "liberty" protected by the due-process clauses of the Fifth and Fourteenth Amendments,[3] to the security of the home provided by the Fourth Amendment,[4] to the freedom of conscience and religion recognized in the First Amendment,[5] to the "privileges and immunities" clause of Article IV and the Fourteenth Amendment,[6] to the "rights . . . retained by the people" under the Ninth Amendment,[7] and, more recently, to "penumbras" emanating from the First, Third, Fourth, Fifth, and Fourteenth Amendments.[8] These constitutional provisions have protected matters as wide-ranging as the right to travel abroad,[9] and the right to conceive (or not to conceive) children,[10] to bear [11] (or not to bear [12]) them, and to rear them as one sees fit.[13]

Federal statutes also provide a measure of protection. The federal Privacy Act of 1974 provides for disclosure to a federal employee or applicant of the reasons he or she is asked to furnish information to the government and the proposed uses of the information.[14] Privacy may also be protected under state law. Some state constitutions expressly grant a right of privacy to their citizens.[15] Additionally, state courts, which are the ultimate arbiters of the meaning of state law, can interpret state constitutional provisions more expansively than their federal analogues. Finally, state and local statutes can protect against matters as varied as the invasion of privacy by a stranger, the misappropriation of identity, and the protection of confidential information.[16]

B. HETEROSEXUAL ASSOCIATIONS

May an unmarried police officer be dismissed for living with a person of the opposite sex?

Probably not.

Courts considering the permissibility of a discreet heterosexual relationship have often found the activities of two unmarried heterosexuals to fall within the zone of privacy that is protected from unwarranted governmental intrusion.[17] Thus, unless it were demonstrated that the officer's living arrangement rendered the officer unfit to do the job—which is unlikely—the officer could not be dismissed for engaging in discreet heterosexual conduct.[18]

Is an unmarried heterosexual relationship still protected if it becomes open and notorious?

Possibly not, depending upon a court's perception of community mores.

On the one hand, a court might find that an unmarried police officer's relationship that became notorious or offensive (such as by exploitation on a television program) reflected a lack of concern for privacy and decorum and undermined the officer's reputation within the community.[19] In such instances, firing the officer would be warranted by the adverse impact of his or her conduct on job performance. On the other hand, an unmarried relationship, albeit highly visible, may comport with community standards and not impair job performance. In such a case, the activity should not serve as a basis for the officer's firing or demotion. Moreover, the right to privacy may protect the officer's relationship. A New Jersey Supreme Court case, *State* v. *Saunders,* struck down an antifornication statute as a violation of the criminal defendant's right of privacy.[20]

May a police officer be dismissed for engaging in an adulterous relationship?

The answer depends upon two factors: (1) the legal status of adultery in the state where the officer resides, and (2) the circumstances surrounding the adultery.

Many states still criminalize adultery (although the

number is decreasing [21]). In states where the police officer's conduct would be a crime, a court might rule that the behavior was incompatible with the officer's public duty to uphold the law or violated public policy and could not be condoned.[22] Even in such instances, however, the court might find the adultery protected if it was only an isolated incident, or remote in time.

More forward-looking courts would do well to eliminate private adulterous acts as a basis for discharge. In the alternative, a court should at the least assess the nature and seriousness of the officer's adultery in terms of the purpose underlying its criminalization. Only in cases where the officer's adultery had destroyed a viable marriage and thus caused the harm which the criminal statute sought to prevent might a court feel justified in upholding sanctions imposed against the police officer.[23]

In jurisdictions where adultery is not criminal, it is more likely that discreet adulterous activity could not serve as a basis for dismissal or demotion.[24] It might remain unprotected, however, were it open and notorious, and so deviant from community norms as to hinder job performance. Such a situation might arise, for example, where an officer is an unbridled "swinger" and exploits his or her activities through the media, inviting public ridicule or disapproval.[25]

C. HOMOSEXUAL ASSOCIATIONS

Does federal law protect a state or city law-enforcement officer against discrimination because of homosexual conduct?

There is no clear answer. The response turns on the statutory and judicial law within a particular officer's jurisdiction.

Although a forceful argument can be made that adult consenting homosexuals should be protected by the Constitution from all governmental interference, such a doctrine has not yet been widely adopted.[26] On the contrary, in *Doe* v. *Commonwealth's Attorney*, the U.S. Supreme Court summarily affirmed the decision of a three-judge district court in Virginia that refused to enjoin the threatened enforcement of a criminal sodomy statute against homosexuals.[27] The district court's reasoning in support of its decision was sparse, and the Supreme Court's summary action, without a written opinion, elucidated little. As such, it is not clear whether *Doe* v. *Commonwealth's Attorney* will have value as a precedent when future cases arise.[28] In fact, the Supreme Court, over Justice Rehnquist's protests, subsequently stated that the issue of sexuality among private consenting adults remains unsettled.[29] Indeed, at least one lower court found that *Doe* is not authoritative on the constitutionality of sodomy statutes.[30]

Because the impact of *Doe* remains unclear, federal as well as state courts can continue to develop the doctrine that employers may not interfere with an employee's homosexual conduct unless it demonstrably affects job performance.[31] Thus, some courts have protected gay employees from dismissals that were considered arbitrary because the employer had shown no connection between job performance and homosexuality.[32] In *Norton* v. *Macy*, decided before *Doe*, Chief Judge Bazelon of the Court of Appeals for the District of Columbia ruled that government employers must show a "nexus" between a person's homosexuality and job performance; adverse personnel action based solely on the status of homosexuality would violate the due-process clause.[33] But as one commentator has noted: "Although the [nexus] test purports to prevent the application of a per se rule of exclusion, it is homosexuality per se that triggers the application of the test." [34] In short, the nexus test provides protection in cases where the employer's reprisals were clearly unrelated to job performance,[35] but where the employer is careful to couch the charges in terms of "unfitness," the test is a meager shield. Some courts have failed to apply even the "unfitness" test, however, and refuse outright to protect the homosexual activity of employees.[36] Accordingly, a state or local officer should consult the federal constitutional law that has developed in the officer's jurisdiction.

As to statutes, there is no federal civil-rights statute that clearly protects homosexual employees. A federal court of appeals has held that Title VII of the 1964 Civil Rights Act, which bars discrimination in employment on the basis of sex and which applies to state and local police departments, does not prohibit discrimination on the basis of sexual preference.[37] The court reasoned that Congress, in enacting Title VII, had only traditional notions of sex and gender in mind. The court further reasoned that employers did not discriminate against male homosexuals on the basis of sex because the employers equally proscribed female homosexuality. Finally, the court concluded that another federal civil-rights statute also did not prohibit discrimination against homosexuals.[38]

Are federal employees protected from discrimination based on homosexual conduct?

Somewhat. In July 1975, the United States Civil Service Commission adopted a regulation prohibiting discrimination against gay employees.[39] The regulation provides that a homosexual can be denied employment "only when the notoriety accompanying the conduct can reasonably be expected to adversely affect" job or agency performance. Furthermore, "unsubstantiated" assertions of "possible embarrassment" cannot substitute for a showing of unfitness. This regulation limits the discretion of employers of civil-service workers only. Employers cannot allege a "nexus" between private homosexual acts and job performance unless the acts are accompanied by "notoriety."

Do state and local laws forbid discrimination against gay police officers?

An increasing number of state and local laws prohibit discrimination based on "sexual orientation" or "affectional preference." Such provisions forbid discrimination in employment against homosexual officers. Jurisdictions that have enacted protective laws include New York City[40]; others, such as Philadelphia, have adopted a policy removing a ban against gay officers.[41] Various university centers have also adopted protective regulations.[42]

Where such laws have not been adopted by local authorities, an officer should consult the case law in the state. The California Supreme Court for example has protected the homosexual's right to employment,[43] even when the employee is arrested for homosexual solicitation,[44] as long as the transgression does not evince "immorality" or "unfitness" to perform on the job. Moreover, the California court has pointed to many legal sources in support of its decisions, including the California Constitution, antidiscrimination clauses in state statutes such as the Public

Utilities Code, and "political activity" provisions in the California Labor Code.[45] Indeed, in a 1979 case involving charges that a public utility discriminated against homosexuals in employment, the California court fashioned a novel theory.[46] It concluded that the "political activity" clause in the state Labor Code extended protection to the gay community's campaign for equal rights: hence the utility could not discriminate against people who identify themselves as homosexuals, who defend homosexuality, or who are identified with activist homosexual organizations. Insofar as the California decision appears to extend protection to activist, "notorious" homosexuals, it breaks new ground.[47]

In contrast to the California Supreme Court, other courts have upheld the discharge of an avowedly homosexual teacher. For instance, in *Gaylord* v. *Tacoma School District No. 10*,[48] the Washington State Supreme Court upheld the dismissal of a school teacher based solely on his status as a homosexual. In order to reverse the dismissal, the court would have required the teacher to prove that he had not committed homosexual acts. Similarly, in *Gish* v. *Board of Education of Paramus*,[49] a New Jersey court declined to reverse a teacher's firing because he had refused to undergo a psychiatric examination after becoming active in a gay-rights organization. One advantage that gay police officers might have over teachers, however, is that courts are very protective of the moral influences on children, a concern not directly applicable to the police.

In sum, state court rulings vary markedly, and should be consulted on a case by case basis.

Does the degree of openness of an officer's homosexuality affect his or her rights? *

Yes, both under federal regulations and under most court decisions. The 1975 Federal Civil Service ruling clearly excludes from protection the situation in which "notoriety" may impair either the individual's fitness or

---

* This and the following question and answer are adapted from Robert O'Neil's *The Rights of Government Employees* (New York: Avon Books, 1978). Minor changes and footnote renumbering are not noted.

the agency's position. Court decisions, too, have often differentiated between private homosexual conduct and flaunted or widely publicized homosexuality (as in the case of a person whose rejection for a library position was upheld by the federal courts on this ground).[50] . . . [Compare, however, the California case discussed in the previous answer which ruled that the advocacy of gay rights is a protected political activity.]

May a public employee forfeit protection by misrepresenting his or her homosexual involvement? *

Yes; so it seems from one important federal court of appeals decision. The case involved a Maryland public school teacher who had been dismissed for being a homosexual. When he sought reinstatement, the court of appeals upheld his substantive claim, finding a constitutionally protected interest in private homosexual activity.[51] The court also held that the teacher could not be discharged because of public statements he had made after his removal, since these were within his freedom of expression. But the teacher ultimately lost because he had lied to school authorities about his homosexuality at the time of his initial employment.[52] Clearly there is a risk either way. If employees conceal their homosexuality, they may later be faced with the charge of lying; if, on the other hand, they make full disclosure when they seek a job, their applications may be rejected.

D. OTHER PERSONAL ASSOCIATIONS

What other kinds of intimate activities may be subject to departmental sanction?

Many courts, notably the California Supreme Court and the Court of Appeals for the District of Columbia,[53] have established the doctrine that an employee's private off-duty conduct cannot be subject to sanction by an employer unless it renders the employee "unfit" to perform the job.[54] Although not unanimous,[55] this rule is increasingly becoming the gauge by which courts assess

* See previous footnote.

whether an employee's conduct is protected. Accordingly, "The courts have increasingly put public agencies to the test of proving a tangible and nontrivial connection between alleged 'immorality' and the employee's ineffectiveness in performing his or her duties." [56]

What factors determine whether a police officer's private activities are rationally related to his or her duties or fitness?

The California Supreme Court offered guidance in *Morrison* v. *State Board of Education*.[57] Though many factors may be examined, depending upon the circumstances of the case, the court referred to the following elements:

the likelihood that the conduct may have adversely affected [the public] or fellow [officers], the degree of such adversity anticipated, the proximity or remoteness in time of the conduct, . . . the extenuating or aggravating circumstances, if any, surrounding the conduct, the praiseworthiness or blameworthiness of the motives resulting in the conduct, [and] the likelihood of the recurrence of the questioned conduct.[58]

Other courts have added the following factors to the balance: the sensitivity of the police position held; the way in which the private conduct relates to that position; society's view of the conduct (including its criminal status); the existence of alternatives that would meet the government's interest without infringing upon the officer's conduct; and the overall record of the officer.[59]

What are some examples of protected sexual or intimate conduct?

One federal district court ruled that an otherwise qualified applicant could not be rejected for employment with the Baltimore police department because he was a member of a nudist organization and spent his weekends in a nudist colony.[60] After satisfying itself that the nudist group was discreet and that the applicant would be able to enforce laws against indecent exposure, the court ruled that "private, nonpolitical association with those who espouse nudism should be no less protected than associations of a political nature." [61]

By analogy, an officer who lives in a commune should not be penalized on the job, unless the officer is violating or could not enforce an ordinance prohibiting such arrangements.[62] Similarly, an aficionado of pornographic materials should not be barred from police work unless he or she is unwilling to enforce antiobscenity statutes.[63] In either example, if the officer's ability to do the job were otherwise somehow impaired, police department disciplinary action would be appropriate.

What are some examples of sexual conduct that would justify disciplinary action?

Perhaps the most common example is sexual activity that involves a husband and wife along with other participants. Here a court would probably find that the married couple's conduct transgressed traditional moral norms and substantially reduced the couple's standing in the community, thus undermining job performance. In *Fabio* v. *Civil Service Commission of Philadelphia,* for example, the Pennsylvania Supreme Court upheld the dismissal of a police officer who induced his wife to have relations with a fellow officer, and who himself had an affair with his wife's sister.[64] The court found the officer's conduct "immoral since Biblical days." Moreover, the court ruled that the officer was not merely a consenting adult engaged in genuinely private conduct, but rather instigated an explosive and disruptive scheme. Thus, the adverse effect of his conduct on his co-workers and family removed it from the protected realm of privacy.

In a different but still relevant factual context, a federal district court ruled that a married couple waived any privacy rights they might have otherwise had by photographing their act of sodomy and allowing the pictures to be viewed by children.[65] The court of appeals affirmed the decision that the couple's activity was not protected, but on the different ground that the couple had invited a stranger (who had answered a magazine advertisement) to observe and maybe participate in their sexual adventure.[66] Another court has ruled that a teacher was validly dismissed from her job when she discussed the experiences of her husband and herself, avowed "swingers," on a local television program.[67] Of course, most private sexual conduct will not come to light unless the officer is careless or an exhibitionist.

E. GROOMING AND DRESS CODES

Do police departments regulate an officer's appearance through grooming and dress codes?

Generally, yes.

"Hair . . . for centuries has been one aspect of the manner in which we hold ourselves out to the rest of the world." [68] Despite the individual expression embodied in personal appearance,[69] many police departments prescribe how an officer should look. The following New York City police regulations are typical:

1. Be neat and clean.
2. Keep uniform clean, well pressed and in good repair.
3. Keep uniform securely buttoned.
4. Wear cap squarely on head, with center of visor directly over nose. . . .
5. Prevent non-uniform articles from showing above uniform collar.
6. Have hair tapered to general shape of head and not reaching collar.
7. Keep sideburns closely trimmed and not extending below bottom of ear lobe. (Gross muttonchops are not permitted.)
8. Have mustaches neatly trimmed, not extending beyond, nor drooping below corners of mouth.
9. Do not grow beards, goatees, etc., except when approved by commanding officer due to nature of member's assignment or when required due to a medical problem and with written approval of Chief Surgeon.
10. Do not wear earrings or other adornments, while performing duty in uniform.[70]

Are police codes that regulate grooming and dress valid?

Yes. In *Kelley* v. *Johnson*,[71] the U.S. Supreme Court upheld the validity of grooming codes used by police departments.

In *Kelley,* the police department of Suffolk County, New York, enacted a regulation that limited hair length, hair style, and the length of sideburns and mustaches. The regulation further forbade the wearing of beards and goatees (except for medical reasons) and wigs (except to cover natural baldness or physical disfiguration). The federal court of appeals that reviewed the case invalidated the hair-length regulation, ruling that the "choice of personal appearance is an ingredient of an individual's personal liberty" protected by the Fourteenth Amendment.[72] The Supreme Court reversed, and upheld the regulation. The Court paid "deference" to "Suffolk County's choice of an organizational structure for its police force." [73] "Here," the Court continued,

> the county has chosen a mode of organization which it undoubtedly deems the most efficient in enabling its police to carry out the duties assigned to them under state and local law. Such a choice necessarily gives weight to the overall need for discipline, esprit de corps, and uniformity.
>
> . . . the hair-length regulation cannot be viewed in isolation but must be rather considered in the context of the county's chosen mode of organization for its police force.
>
> The promotion of safety of persons and property is unquestionably at the core of the State's police power, and virtually all state and local governments employ a uniformed police force to aid in the accomplishment of that purpose. Choice of organization, dress, and equipment for law enforcement personnel is a decision entitled to the same sort of presumption of legislative validity as are state choices designed to promote other aims within the cognizance of the State's police power. . . . Thus the question is not, as the Court of Appeals conceived it to be, whether the State can "establish" a "genuine public need" for the specific regulation. It is whether [the officer] can demonstrate that there is no *rational connection* between the regulation, based as it is on the county's method of organizing its police force, and the promotion of safety of persons and property. . . .[74]

The Court readily found the "rational connection" required to justify the grooming regulation:

> The overwhelming majority of state and local police of the present day are uniformed. This fact itself testifies to the recognition by those who direct those operations, and by the people of the states and localities who directly or indirectly choose such persons, that similarity in appearance of police officers is desirable. This choice may be based on a desire to make police officers readily recognizable to the members of the public, or a desire for the esprit de corps which such similarity is felt to inculcate within the police force itself. Either one is a sufficiently rational justification for regulations so as to defeat [the officer's] claim based on the liberty guarantee of the Fourteenth Amendment.[75]

Although some may find it difficult to "connect" the length of sideburns with the ability to "recognize" a uniformed and badged officer, or with officer morale ("espirit de corps"), *Kelley* represents the state of the law.

Does *Kelley v. Johnson* permit the regulation of other matters pertaining to appearance and manner, such as courtesy and smoking in public while uniformed?

Yes. The Supreme Court's reasoning in *Kelley* makes it clear that matters of appearance and manner can be regulated unless so "irrational" as to be "branded 'arbitrary.' "[76] Indeed, the *Kelley* Court expressly mentioned requirements of appearance and behavior other than grooming codes, and implied that they too are permissible. Although these regulations ranged from the important to the trivial, the Court did not distinguish among them, explaining that as law-enforcement personnel, police officers are subject to "demands . . . which have no counterpart with respect to the public at large."[77]

The *Kelley* Court obviously sanctioned the wearing of "a standard uniform, specific in each detail."[78] An officer can be compelled to sport the required dress, wear a helmet,[79] satisfy neatness standards, and display the requisite insignia. Moreover, one state court has held that officers can be ordered to wear a flag patch on their sleeve,[80] even though this requirement appears to force avowal of a set political or philosophical view. If flag-wearing can be required, undoubtedly officers can be compelled to exhibit name tags, badges, and the like,[81] since unlike a forced flag display, these displays barely implicate First Amendment interests. The *Kelley* Court also impliedly sanctioned required flag salutes.[82] Although such an order would violate the First Amendment if applied to the citizenry at large, members of a law-enforcement corps can be compelled to conform to a greater standard of discipline and uniformity.[83]

Furthermore, officers can be ordered to use required "equipment," [84] which would include the prescribed firearms and other dangerous devices, unless the requirement were arbitrary.[85] Regulations forbidding smoking in public while uniformed also received the Court's blessing.[86] By analogy, a department can reasonably regulate matters of propriety and courtesy, ranging from tipping a hat to respectfully addressing the public.

In short, in light of *Kelly*'s broad approval of the governmental interest in maintaining morale and uniformity among officers, it is hard to conceive of a rule of behavior or grooming that could not be justified as enhancing morale or discipline.

F. PROCEDURAL PROTECTIONS

May a police officer be compelled to answer questions about private sexual associations?

Yes, but only if the questions are properly drawn and are related to the officer's job performance.

Courts have recognized that the government has a legitimate interest in ascertaining the fitness of its employees. Thus, the government may ask questions that are reasonably related to its interests as an employer. The government may not embark on a fishing expedition, however. Nor may it legitimize its questions merely by including them as part of an "official investigation" under a long-standing, well-known police policy.[87] Rather the government may ask questions only if they are clear, relatively precise, and reasonably limited in scope.[88] They should also be appropriately directed to the person being questioned.

Finally, they should be rationally related to the police officer's duties or fitness.

Moreover, there must be a legitimate basis for inquiring into the particular area of conduct. For example, a police department could not ask randomly selected applicants detailed questions about sexual activity. Rather it could only inquire when it had some reasonable suspicion that sexual conduct that was related to job performance was implicated.

Are regulations prohibiting "conduct unbecoming an officer" or "conduct prejudicial to good order" valid?

Since courts are sharply divided, there is no clear answer to this increasingly important issue.

Many local ordinances [89] and police regulations [90] prohibit "immoral conduct," "conduct unbecoming an officer," or "conduct prejudicial to good order and efficiency." Indeed, under such prohibitions officers have been dismissed for engaging in conduct as diverse as shooting deer out of season and without a license,[91] visiting an illegal gambling club,[92] accepting three checks of $3.00 each from a local lawyer,[93] and making improper advances to a woman acquaintance.[94] The law is evolving so that police officers must be reasonably warned of what conduct is objectionable before they can be penalized for it.[95] In a landmark opinion, a three-judge panel of the Court of Appeals for the Fifth Circuit invalidated a fire department regulation and city ordinance prohibiting "conduct prejudicial to good order." [96] The panel found many infirmities in the law. First, the law potentially inhibited protected speech or protected political activity under the First Amendment. Second, it could not be justified on the outmoded theory that a public employee is subject to discharge at whim. Third, there were no limiting regulations or body of doctrine which could give guidance in interpreting the meaning and scope of the law. The panel thus concluded that standards such as "conduct prejudicial to good order" "are both vague and overbroad absent limitation or guidance regarding their scope;" accordingly, administrators must adopt minimum standards or guidelines that make clear the duties and responsibilities of public employees and protect their rights as citizens. The Fifth Circuit panel opinion was reversed in a decision by the entire court. The *en banc* majority held that catch-all provisions such as the one before the court give the only type of notice that can practically and effectively be given for unspecified or as yet unimagined misbehavior. Seven judges dissented, agreeing with the panel.

In a vein similar to the Fifth Circuit panel opinion, the Court of Appeals for the District of Columbia Circuit invalidated Air Force regulations that required the discharge of homosexuals "unless the most unusual circumstances" exist.[97] The court reasoned that the absence of articulated standards, coupled with the absence of a reasoned explanation by the Air Force justifying the particular discharge at issue, made impossible any meaningful judicial review of whether the discharge constituted an abuse of the Air Force's discretion. The court of appeals decision stands for the proposition that disciplinary or dismissal measures must be accompanied both by overall articulated standards as well as by a rational explanation justifying the particular measure taken. By analogy, proscriptions against "unbecoming" or "prejudicial" conduct by an officer are not valid unless articulated in advance and relevant to the particular course of conduct.

The reasoning of the District of Columbia Circuit has not been followed in the Fifth Circuit or in some other jurisdictions, however. The police officer who was dismissed for violating game laws had petitioned his state's highest court and the Supreme Court of the United States for a decision that statutes prohibiting conduct "unbecoming an officer," "tending to destroy public respect," and "adversely affecting police morale" did not present him with a fair warning that his acts were punishable.[98] The Pennsylvania Supreme Court afforded him no relief, and the United States Supreme Court refused to review the case.[99]

NOTES

1. *See* L. TRIBE, AMERICAN CONSTITUTIONAL LAW §15–13, at 941–42 n. 3 (1978) [hereinafter TRIBE].
2. Olmstead v. United States, 277 U.S. 438, 478 (1928) (Brandeis, J., dissenting).
3. Roe v. Wade, 410 U.S. 113, 153 (1973).

4. *See* Olmstead v. United States, 277 U.S. 438, 478 (1928) (Brandeis, G., dissenting).

5. TRIBE §§15–5 to 15–8; §15–20, at 984–85.

6. *See* Doe v. Bolton, 410 U.S. 179, 200 (1973).

7. *See* Redlich, *Are There Certain Rights . . . Retained by the People?*, 37 N.Y.U.L. REV. 787 (1962).

8. *See* Whalen v. Roe, 429 U.S. 589, 598 n. 23 (1977). *See generally* TRIBE §15–3, at 893–94.

9. Kent v. Dulles, 357 U.S. 116 (1958).

10. Eisenstadt v. Baird, 405 U.S. 438 (1972).

11. Cleveland Bd. of Educ. v. LaFleur, 414 U.S. 632 (1974).

12. Roe v. Wade, 410 U.S. 113 (1973).

13. Pierce v. Society of Sisters, 268 U.S. 510 (1925).

14. Act of Dec. 31, 1974, Pub. L. No. 93–579, 88 Stat. 1896 (codified at 5 U.S.C. §552a).

15. Alaska Const. art. I, §22 ("The right of the people to privacy is recognized and shall not be infringed").

16. TRIBE §15–3, at 895.

17. *E.g.*, Shuman v. City of Philadelphia, 47 U.S.L.W. 2720 (E.D. Pa. Apr. 18, 1979). *Cf.* City of Santa Barbara v. Adamson, 48 U.S.L.W. 2783 (Cal. Sup. Ct. May 15, 1980) (ordinance prohibiting more than five unrelated persons from living together violates privacy guarantees of California Constitution).

18. *Cf.* Carter v. United States, 407 F.2d 1238 (D.C. Cir. 1968).

19. *See* Pettit v. State Bd. of Educ., 10 Cal. 3d 29, 513 P.2d 889, 109 Cal. Rptr. 665 (1973). *Cf.* Hollenbaugh v. Carnegie Free Library, 436 F. Supp. 1328 (W.D. Pa. 1977), *aff'd*, 578 F.2d 1374 (3d Cir.) (en banc), *cert. denied*, 439 U.S. 1052 (1978); Sedule v. Capital School Dist., 425 F. Supp. 552 (D. Del. 1976), *aff'd*, 565 F.2d 153 (3d Cir. 1977), *cert. denied*, 434 U.S. 1037 (1978).

20. 75 N.J. 200, 381 A.2d 333 (1977). *Cf.* City of Santa Barbara v. Adamson, 48 U.S.L.W. 2783 (Cal. Sup. Ct. May 15, 1980) (ordinance prohibiting more than five unrelated persons from living together violates privacy guarantees of California Constitution).

21. *See, e.g.*, P.A. No. 828, [1969] Conn. P.A. 1618, *repealing* Conn. Gen. Stat. §53–218 (West 1960) (repealing criminal adultery statute).

22. *Cf.* McCall v. Frampton, 415 N.Y.S. 2d 752 (Sup. Ct. 1979).

23. *Cf.* Moon Ho Kim v. INS, 514 F.2d 179, 181 (D.C. Cir. 1975); Wadman v. INS, 329 F.2d 812 (9th Cir. 1964).

24. *See* Erb v. Iowa State Bd. of Publ. Instruction, 216 N.W.2d 339 (Iowa 1974) (teacher who committed adultery held "morally fit to teach").

25. *See* Pettit v. State Bd. of Educ., 10 Cal. 3d 29, 513 P.2d 889, 109 Cal. Rptr. 665 (1973) (married teacher dismissed as active "swinger" who described her activities on television program).

26. *See* TRIBE §15–13, at 943, *citing* Gerety, *Redefining Privacy*, 12 HARV. C.R.-C.L. L. REV. 233, 280–81 (1977). *Accord,* New York v. Onofre, 48 U.S.L.W. 2520 (N.Y. App. Div. Jan. 24, 1980).

27. 425 U.S. 901 (1976), *summarily aff'g* 403 F. Supp. 1199 (E.D. Va. 1975).

28. TRIBE §15–13, at 943.

29. Carey v. Population Serv. Int'l, 431 U.S. 678, 694 n. 17 (1977).

30. *See* State v. Pilcher, 242 N.W.2d 348 (Iowa 1976) (application of sodomy law to consenting unmarried heterosexuals violates privacy and equal-protection rights). *Compare id. with* Lovisi v. Slayton, 539 F.2d 349, 352 (4th Cir. 1965) (en banc), *cert. denied,* 429 U.S. 977 (1977), Matlovich v. Secretary of Air Force, 414 F. Supp. 690 (D.D.C. 1976), *vacated and remanded,* 591 F.2d 852 (D.C. Cir. 1978) (court of appeals ruled that Air Force must articulate reasons for discharging homosexual member), *and* Berg v. Claytor, 591 F.2d 849 (D.C. Cir. 1978) (companion case with Matlovich). *But cf.* Beller v. Middendorf, 49 U.S.L.W. 2289 (9th Cir. Oct. 23, 1980) (interpreting *Doe* to mean that homosexuality does not enjoy special constitutional protection).

31. *E.g.,* New York v. Onofre, 48 U.S.L.W. 2520 (N.Y. App. Div. Jan. 24, 1980) (consensual sodomy statute disallowing "deviate" intercourse held to violate constitutional right to privacy).

32. Ben Shalom v. Secretary of Army, 48 U.S.L.W. 2778 (E.D. Wis. May 20, 1980) (Army discharge of soldier who evidences homosexual "tendencies, desire or interest" but not acts violates First Amendment rights of association and expression, Fifth Amendment, and right of privacy protected by First and Ninth amendments; sexual preferences cannot be controlled absent nexus between preference and soldier's military capabilities); Saal v.

Middendorf, 427 F. Supp. 192 (N.D. Cal. 1977); Society for Individual Rights, Inc. v. Hampton, 63 F.R.D. 399 (N.D. Cal. 1973), *aff'd on other grounds*, 528 F.2d 905 (9th Cir. 1975). *See* Norton v. Macy, 417 F.2d 1161 (D.C. Cir. 1969). *See generally* 1978 Ann. Survey Am. L. 455.

33. 417 F.2d 1161, 1164 (D.C. Cir. 1969).

34. 1978 Ann. Survey Am. L. 455, 457.

35. Aumiller v. University of Del., 434 F. Supp. 1273 (D. Del. 1977).

36. *E.g.*, Gaylord v. Tacoma School Dist. No. 10, 88 Wash. 2d 286, 559 P.2d 1340 (en banc), *cert. denied*, 434 U.S. 879 (1977); Singer v. United States Civil Serv. Comm'n, 530 F.2d 247 (9th Cir. 1976), *vacated in light of new regulations*, 429 U.S. 1034 (1977). *See* Beller v. Middendorf, 49 U.S.L.W. 2289 (9th Cir. Oct. 23, 1980) (upholding Navy regulations requiring discharge of gays).

37. Desantis v. Pacific Tel. & Tel. Co., 608 F.2d 327 (9th Cir. 1979).

38. 42 U.S.C. §1985(3).

39. *See* 44 U.S.L.W. 2032 (U.S. Civ. Serv. Comm'n, FPM Ltr. 731–3 July 3, 1975). *Cf.* Neaveill v. Andolsek, 577 F.2d 749 (7th Cir.) (aff'g mem. unreported district court opinion), *summarized* at 47 U.S.L.W. 3253 (No. 78–315) (off-duty conduct of U.S. Postal Service Security officer rationally found to have adverse effect on efficiency of postal service), *cert. denied*, 439 U.S. 965 (1978).

40. City of New York Exec. Ord. No. 4, §1 (Jan. 23, 1978) ("There shall be no discrimination by any City administration, agency, department, commission or other official entity, or any official representative thereof, on account of sexual orientation or affectional preference in any matter of hiring or employment, housing, credit, contracting, provision of services, or any other matter whatsoever"). *See* R. O'NEIL, THE RIGHTS OF GOVERNMENT EMPLOYEES 119–20 (1978).

41. N.Y. Times, Aug. 8, 1980 ("Police in Philadelphia Lift Homosexual Ban").

42. O'NEIL, *supra* note 40 at 119–20.

43. Gay Law Students Ass'n v. Pacific Tel. & Tel. Co., 24 Cal. 3d 458, 595 P.2d 592, 156 Cal. Rptr. 14 (1979); Board of Educ. v. Jack M., 19 Cal. 3d 691, 566 P.2d 602, 139 Cal. Rptr. 700 (1977) (en banc); Morrison v. State

Bd. of Educ., 1 Cal. 3d 214, 461 P.2d 375, 82 Cal. Rptr. 175 (1969) (en banc).

44. Board of Educ. v. Jack M., 19 Cal. 3d 691, 566 P.2d 602, 139 Cal. Rptr. 700 (1977) (en banc).

45. Gay Law Students Ass'n v. Pacific Tel. & Tel. Co., 24 Cal. 3d 458, 595 P.2d 592, 156 Cal. Rptr. 14 (1979).

46. *Id.*

47. *See also* Gay Lib v. University of Mo., 558 F.2d 848 (8th Cir. 1977), *cert. denied,* 434 U.S. 1080 (1978) (recognizing First Amendment rights of "gay consciousness" group, outside employment setting).

48. 88 Wash. 2d 286, 559 P.2d 1340 (en banc), *cert. denied,* 434 U.S. 879 (1977).

49. 145 N.J. Super. 96, 366 A.2d 1337 (1976), *petition for cert. denied,* 74 N.J. 251, 377 A.2d 658 (1977), *cert. denied,* 434 U.S. 879 (1978).

50. McConnell v. Anderson, 451 F.2d 193 (8th Cir. 1971), *cert. denied,* 405 U.S. 1046 (1972).

51. Acanfora v. Board of Educ., 491 F.2d 498 (4th Cir. 1974).

52. *Id.* at 504.

53. California: Morrison v. State Bd. of Educ., 1 Cal. 3d 214, 461 P.2d 375, 82 Cal. Rptr. 175 (1969) (en banc). D.C. Court of Appeals: Norton v. Macy, 417 F.2d 1161 (D.C. Cir. 1969).

54. Tribe §15–13, at 941–42 n. 3. *See* Herzbrun v. Milwaukee County, 338 F. Supp. 736, 738 (E.D. Wis. 1972).

55. *See* Tribe §15–13, at 941–42 n. 3.

56. *Id.*

57. 1 Cal. 3d 214, 461 P.2d 375, 82 Cal. Rptr. 175 (1969).

58. 1 Cal. 3d at 229, 461 P.2d at 386, 82 Cal. Rptr. at 186 (footnotes omitted).

59. *See* O'Neil, *The Private Lives of Public Employees,* 51 Ore. L. Rev. 70, 102–12 (1971).

60. Bruns v. Pomerlau, 319 F. Supp. 58 (D. Md. 1970).

61. *Id.* at 68.

62. *Cf.* Village of Belle Terre v. Borasas, 416 U.S. 1 (1974). *But see* note 17 *supra.*

63. *Cf.* Stanley v. Georgia, 394 U.S. 557 (1969) (private viewing of obscene materials in one's home is constitutionally protected).

64. 48 U.S.L.W. 2752 (Pa. Apr. 30, 1980).

65. Lovisi v. Slayton, 363 F. Supp. 621 (E.D. Va. 1973),

aff'd on other grounds, 539 F.2d 349 (4th Cir. 1976) (en banc), *cert. denied,* 429 U.S. 977 (1977).

66. *Id.*
67. *See* Pettit v. State Bd. of Educ., 10 Cal. 2d 29, 513 P.2d 889, 109 Cal. Rptr. 665 (1975).
68. Karr v. Schmidt, 460 F.2d 609, 621 (5th Cir.) (en banc) (Wisdom, J., dissenting), *cert. denied,* 409 U.S. 989 (1972).
69. TRIBE §15–16 at 959, *citing* Ham v. South Carolina, 409 U.S. 524, 529–30 (1973) (Douglas, J., dissenting), *and* Arnold v. Carpenter, 459 F.2d 939 (7th Cir. 1972).
70. New York City Police Dep't Patrol Guide, Proc. No. 104–1, at 3 (effective Aug. 25, 1976).
71. 425 U.S. 238 (1976). *Accord,* Ablondi v. Framingham Police Dep't. —— Mass. App. —— (Apr. 17, 1979), *cited in Boston Globe,* Apr. 18, 1979, at 19.
72. 483 F.2d 1126, 1130 (2d Cir. 1973).
73. 425 U.S. at 246.
74. *Id.* at 246–47 (footnotes and citations omitted).
75. *Id.* at 248. A survey taken in Framingham, Massachusetts, "showed that 90 percent of young people considered neatness important for police, and 87 percent considered appearance important for police to gain public respect." Boston Globe, Apr. 18, 1979, at 19.
76. 425 U.S. at 248.
77. *Id* at 245.
78. *Id.*
79. *Cf.* State v. Odegaard, 165 N.W.2d 677 (N.D. 1969); State *ex rel.* Colvin v. Lombardi, 241 A.2d 625, 627 (R.I. 1968).
80. Slocum v. Fire & Police Comm'n, 8 Ill. App. 2d 465, 290 N.E.2d 28 (1972).
81. *See id.*
82. 425 U.S. at 245–46.
83. *See id.* at 244–46, 248–49.
84. *Id.* at 247.
85. For a discussion of the right to protest unduly dangerous working conditions, *see* Chapter IX, Section C.
86. 425 U.S. at 246.
87. Shuman v. City of Philadelphia, 47 U.S.L.W. 2720 (E.D. Pa. Apr. 14, 1979).
88. *See id.*
89. *E.g.,* N.Y.C. AD. CODE §434a–13.0.
90. *E.g.,* New York City Police Dep't Patrol Guide, Proc.

No. 104–1, at p. 2 ("Prohibited Conduct No. 3") (December 22, 1978). *See* Fabio v. Civil Serv. Comm'n, 48 U.S.L.W. 2752 (Pa. Apr. 30, 1980).

91. Comly v. Township of Lower Southampton, 27 Pa. Comm. 202, 365 A.2d 883 (1976), *aff'd*, 46 U.S.L.W. 3104 (Pa. 1977), *cert. denied*, 434 U.S. 821 (1978).

92. *See* Fabio v. Civil Service Comm'n, 48 U.S.L.W. 2752 (Pa. Apr. 30, 1980).

93. Smith v. Valentine, 282 N.Y. 351, 26 N.E.2d 288 (1940).

94. *See* Fabio v. Civil Serv. Comm'n, 48 U.S.L.W. 2752 (Pa. Apr. 30, 1980).

95. Davis v. Williams, 588 F.2d 69 (5th Cir. 1979), *rev'd en banc*, 48 U.S.L.W. 2814 (5th Cir. May 19, 1980), *cert. denied*, 49 U.S.L.W. 3289 (U.S. Oct. 20, 1980) (No. 80–275). Carter v. United States, 407 F.2d 901 (7th Cir. 1970). Zekas v. Baldwin, 334 F. Supp. 1158 (E.D. Wis. 1970). *See* Muller v. Conlisk, 429 F.2d 901 (7th Cir. 1970).

96. Davis v. Williams, 588 F.2d 69 (5th Cir. 1979), *rev'd en banc*, 48 U.S.L.W. 2814 (5th Cir. May 19, 1980), *cert. denied*, 49 U.S.L.W. 3289 (U.S. Oct. 20, 1980) (No. 80–275).

97. Matlovich v. Secretary of Air Force, 519 F.2d 852 (D.C. Cir. 1978).

98. Comly v. Township of Lower Southampton, 27 Pa. Comm. 202, 365 A.2d 883 (1976), *aff'd*, 46 U.S.L.W. 3104 (Pa. 1977), *cert. denied*, 434 U.S. 821 (1978).

99. *Id. See also* Fabio v. Civil Serv. Comm'n, 48 U.S.L.W. 2752 (Pa. Apr. 30, 1980) (officer dismissed for engaging in disruptive adulterous conduct had been given fair warning that his conduct was "unbecoming an officer").

VI

Procedural Due-Process Rights

Under the Fifth and Fourteenth Amendments of the U.S. Constitution, neither the federal government nor the states may "deprive any person of life, liberty, or property, without due process of law." To judge if a police officer's right to due process has been violated by departmental action, and to help structure police-department mechanisms to give appropriate procedural protections, two questions must be answered. First, are an officer's property or liberty interests impaired? If so, the Constitution requires procedural safeguards for these interests. Second, how much process is due? That is, what particular safeguards are required in a given case?

Depending on the circumstances, an officer might be entitled to a full opportunity to present his or her case before any adverse action is taken, or simply to an after-the-fact written explanation from the department. Whatever safeguards are required, however, the government employer must further differentiate among (1) the procedures required before it takes adverse personnel action, (2) the protections applicable after it takes action, and (3) the proceedings necessary if it publicly reveals its reasons for the action. The first and second sets of procedures relate generally to the employee's interest in keeping his or her job, or "property" under the Constitution; the third relates to the employee's interest in his or her reputation, or "liberty," under the Constitution.

If a property interest is impaired, must the police department provide some procedural protection to the officer?

Yes. The difficult issue, however, is defining when a constitutionally protected property interest in one's job has been abridged, such as by firing, suspension, or demotion. Generally speaking, a police officer must have a "legitimate claim of entitlement" or right to his or her job before the officer will be considered to have a property interest requiring due process.[1] Whether an officer has such an entitlement depends on state property law, not federal constitutional law.

For example, in *Bishop* v. *Wood*, a police officer claimed a constitutional right to a pretermination hearing on the ground that he was classified as a permanent employee under a Marion, North Carolina, town ordinance.[2] The officer had become a permanent employee after six months' probationary service. He claimed that his classification as permanent raised "a sufficient expectancy of continued employment to constitute a protected property interest." The Supreme Court rejected this claim, holding that since a property interest is created by state (not federal) law and since the Marion ordinance had been interpreted to create an employment relationship that was terminable at the will and pleasure of the city, the officer's discharge did not abridge any legitimate expectation that his position would continue.

There are three lessons to be learned from this aspect of the *Bishop* case. First, an officer's property interest is determined by state property and employment laws. Accordingly, the property rights of an officer (and thus his or her procedural due-process rights) will depend on his or her state's statutes and case law. (As an example, the highest court of New Jersey recently upheld the common-law right of employees in that state not to be fired for refusing to act in a way that clearly violates New Jersey law and public policy.[3]) As a corollary of following state property law, the U.S. Supreme Court has given the states freedom to minimize their procedural obligations by writing employment statutes that can be interpreted narrowly by the state's courts. If a state's laws reduce or eliminate its employees' property interests in their jobs, then procedural safeguards will be inapplicable. One commentator has strongly criticized *Bishop* as a "narrowly formalistic approach, relying on verbal distinctions having no relation to reasonable expectations or to public understandings, [and that] seems far too obscure to serve the purposes of protecting reliance on government, reducing helplessness, or enhancing accountability." [4] For federal employees, on the other hand, federal statutes and federal court interpretations will determine the property rights attaching to federal employment.

Second, to the extent that state governments deny procedural protections, employees may lose their opportunity to challenge the truth and adequacy of the government's stated reasons for its adverse action. The *Bishop* Court said that the employee's "constitutionally protected interest in liberty is no greater even if we assume that the City Manager deliberately lied." [5] In other words, because Bishop had no state right to question the adequacy of the cause of his dismissal, the truth or falsity of his superiors' reasoning could not be challenged on constitutional grounds. The Court went on to say that a false justification for a firing "might conceivably provide the basis for a state-law claim, the validity of which would be entirely unaffected by our analysis of the federal constitutional question." [6]

Bishop's third lesson strikes a somewhat more hopeful note. It involves what lawyers call "forum allocation"— the distribution of legal claims primarily between federal courts and state courts and legislatures. Although the Supreme Court clearly is taking a narrow, formal approach to property and procedural rights, it has never denied the importance of the citizen's interests. Instead, the Court appears to wish to leave state-employee relations in the state courts and legislatures. Cases like *Bishop* give states the opportunity to cut back on procedural protections, but whether they will ignore employees' substantial stakes in their jobs is open to question. Although the states may grant some level of protection, maybe even a high level, to police officers, no uniform minimum standards will apply nationwide.

Is dismissal the only infringement of property rights that requires procedural safeguards?

No, but in accordance with *Bishop* v. *Wood*, the key determinant is still state property law. If state property law creates a legitimate claim of entitlement to a specific position, then a suspension, a demotion, or a transfer will also call into question the police officer's property interest.[7]

If a liberty interest is called into question, must the police department afford some protective procedures?

Yes, but again the difficult issue is determining when a constitutionally-protected liberty interest is at stake. Part of the "right to be let alone" is the right to avoid public disclosure of embarrassing private facts and public exposure that depicts a person in a false light.[8] These rights, which relate to reputation, are part of the liberty interest which governments are apt to infringe when they reveal the reasons for taking adverse action against police officers. These infringements on reputation must be considered separately from property losses.

In *Bishop* v. *Wood*, the officer was fired without a hearing.[9] He was told the reasons for his firing orally and in private; it was only during pretrial discovery that he received a written explanation that "his dismissal was based on a failure to follow certain orders, poor attendance at police training classes, causing low morale, and conduct unsuited to an officer." [10] One of the police officer's contentions was that the reasons given for his discharge deprived him of his constitutionally protected liberty because they constituted "a stigma that may severely damage his reputation in the community" and because the reasons given were false.[11] In evaluating the police officer's contentions, the Supreme Court accepted for the sake of argument the officer's version of the facts: "that he was a competent police officer; that he was respected by his peers; that he made more arrests than any other officer on the force; that although he had been criticized for engaging in high-speed pursuits, he had promptly heeded such criticism; and that he had a reasonable explanation for his imperfect attendance at police training sessions." [12]

Nevertheless, the Supreme Court rejected the police officer's claim that his dismissal violated a liberty interest by creating a reputation-damaging stigma. The Court reasoned that because the dismissal decision was communicated to the officer orally and in private there was no basis for a claim of impaired reputation. The department's reasons for firing the officer became public only when his lawyer formally requested them during the lawsuit, well after the firing. Thus, a discharge of a police officer without a hearing will not violate the officer's liberty interest protected by the due-process clause of the Fourteenth

Amendment where the officer is informed privately of the reasons for the discharge or where the reasons for the discharge become public as part of the judicial process.

In another case, *Codd* v. *Velger,* a New York City police officer who was fired alleged that he was entitled to a hearing because of the "stigmatizing effect of certain material placed by the City Police Department in his personnel file." [13] He contended that the department caused his dismissal from a subsequent job with a private police agency by releasing the derogatory information to his new employer. The employer had received a written authorization from Velger to review the file. This release of information was to a more limited audience than was the disclosure in *Bishop,* but it was also more likely to have a direct effect on Velger's employment.

The circuit court ruled that a hearing was required before releasing Velger's personnel information. The court also found Velger's consent to release of his file to the new employer ineffective "since former employees had no practical alternative but to consent . . . if they wished to be seriously considered for other employment." [14]

On review, the Supreme Court reversed, concluding that, where an employee has no property right in forcing the government to justify the reasons for a dismissal, he can demand a hearing to challenge the subsequent release of personnel information only "if the employer creates and disseminates a *false and defamatory* impression about the employee in connection with his termination." [15] Thus, *Codd* v. *Velger* clarified the difference between challenging a termination and challenging the release of information. In another context the Court held that persons who allege that they have been stigmatized by government disclosures have no right to a hearing to preserve reputation *alone.*[16] However, where a government employee can show actual injury—firing from the new job—in addition to damage to reputation, the Court may be willing to require a hearing.[17] To be accorded such a hearing, a plaintiff must assert that the information released is "false and defamatory." [18] In *Codd* v. *Velger,* the plaintiff never challenged "the substantial accuracy of the material in question." [19] Accordingly, the Court held that "the absence of any such allegation or finding [was] fatal to [the officer's] claim under the Due Process Clause that he should have been given a hearing." [20]

When a property interest is called into question, what procedures must be established to safeguard the individual officer's constitutional rights?

In general terms, the types of procedures that will be required by the due-process clause are measured by three factors set forth in *Mathews* v. *Eldridge:*

> . . . First, the private interest that will be affected by the official action; second, the risk of an erroneous deprivation of such interest through the procedures used, and the probable value, if any, of additional or substitute procedural safeguards; and finally, the Government's interest, including the function involved and the fiscal and administrative burdens that the additional or substitute procedural requirement would entail.[21]

In *Mathews,* the Court dealt with the due process required for terminating disability-insurance payments and upheld "a procedure that relied on initial written submissions, followed by pretermination knowledge of the reasons for the action and an opportunity to submit additional arguments and evidence in writing," as well as a post-termination "evidentiary, but nonadversary, hearing at which [the recipient] could be represented by counsel." [22] Under the *Mathews* formulation, it is unlikely that police officers can compel greater procedural protection than that actually afforded in *Mathews.* This is especially true in light of the statement in *Mathews* recognizing that "in contrast to the discharged . . . employee . . . , there is little possibility that the terminated recipient will be able to find even temporary employment to ameliorate the interim loss." [23] Because a discharged or disciplined police officer is in a less disadvantageous position than a terminated disability-insurance recipient, it is hard to believe that, as a matter of constitutional law, a police department can be required to grant more extensive procedural safeguards than those afforded in *Mathews.* And it is possible that the constitutional minimum required may be less substantial than the procedures afforded in *Mathews.*

Is the result different when a liberty interest is involved?

Perhaps, depending on the circumstances. Arguably, if a police officer were fired in a publicly stigmatizing fashion prior to a "name-clearing" evidentiary hearing, a post-termination hearing might be inadequate since the loss of liberty may already have occurred. In the case of a deprivation of property rights, the opportunity to rectify the deprivation is likely to be greater.

Is notice to police officers of impending adverse personnel action required?

Yes, at least whenever some further procedural safeguard is required. Thus, where a hearing is required or even where only a written statement is mandated, some form of notice indicating the nature of the charges against the police officer must be given. The notice must be in such form that the charges are understandable and provide a basis for the officer to seek to rebut them.[24]

Are there some circumstances where a police officer may compel a pretermination hearing?

Yes. First, if the agency's own rules provide for a pretermination hearing, the guarantee may not be withdrawn or curtailed in individual cases. The Supreme Court has held many times that a government agency is bound to follow its own rules, even where the procedures provided by those rules may not be constitutionally required.[25]

Second, a post-termination hearing would suffice only if the agency provides some opportunity to contest the decision before it takes effect—at the very least, a chance to know the reasons for the decision and to dispute them before a responsible agency official.[26] (There may, of course, be "emergency" situations, such as that involving strikes by firefighters and police officers, where even such interim procedures as these can be dispensed with in the interest of protecting the public safety.[27])

Third, the post-termination evidentiary hearing must be at a "meaningful" time—that is, soon after the discharge, since a long delay could deny any meaningful relief to the unemployed person.

The employee who eventually prevails is often reinstated with back pay and other retroactive benefits.

Such a provision is no substitute for a hearing before dismissal, but at least makes the post-termination appeal more acceptable.

Does due process include access to an impartial decision-maker? *

Yes, but that does not require that the person have had no prior involvement with the case. Courts have universally recognized that due process requires an impartial, unbiased forum. A person who has already made up his or her mind about the case—in one instance, by having hired a permanent replacement for the employee who was appealing—is not able to judge the case objectively. But not every degree of involvement will disqualify a decision-maker. Quite recently, the Supreme Court considered the question of whether a school board can impartially review the dismissals of teachers engaged in a strike against the board. The teachers had argued that such a hearing denied them due process for two reasons: (1) because the board had a stake in the outcome of the strike, and (2) because the board was in fact a participant in the negotiations that precipitated the discharge of the striking teachers. The Supreme Court rejected both claims, and held that the board could serve as an impartial hearing body.[28] First, the Court ruled that the school board lacked "the kind of personal and financial stake in the decision that might create a conflict of interest" even though the strike had created some bitterness in the community. The Court also held that "mere familiarity with the facts of a case gained by an agency in the performance of its statutory role does not . . . disqualify a decision maker." Nor, said the majority, is an agency unfairly biased because it has previously taken a public position on the issue involved in the discharge, without proof that it is incapable of judging the particular controversy fairly. Thus, despite the fact that the board had triggered the discharge and that the negotiations were still going on, the Court held that due process had been satisfied.

Several factors in this case may temper the force of the

* This question is reproduced from Robert O'Neil's *The Rights of Government Employees* (New York: Avon Books, 1978).

decision. For one thing, the strike was illegal under Wisconsin law, and the substantive issue was thus unusually clear and narrow. Moreover, the state laws gave the school board very explicit powers with respect to both the dismissal of teachers and the management of the school district—powers that in the Supreme Court's view would have been seriously undermined if the board could not act as the hearing body. Also, as a practical matter, there were no obvious alternatives. Even the state supreme court, which found the school board biased, could only suggest that the board render an initial decision, subject to review by a court. In the absence of some better alternative designed by the legislature, the state court felt powerless to provide an alternative forum for review of teacher dismissals.

May police departments afford greater protection than that required by the Constitution?

Yes. The Constitution sets minimum standards with which police departments must comply. Certainly, they may give more procedural protections. For example, a New York City police officer who is to be fined or reprimanded is entitled to written charges. The charges must then be examined, heard, and investigated by the Police Commissioner or by a deputy upon reasonable notice to the officer.[29]

Are some positions in the public service "above" or "beyond" due process? *

At certain levels in the public service, courts would be far less inclined to probe the dismissal process. For example, persons holding "policy-making" positions may be dismissed for partisan political reasons, even though the Supreme Court has held that patronage dismissal of routine public employees abridges First Amendment rights.[30] On this basis, a court would probably be less likely to order a hearing in the case of a high-ranking policy-maker since the need for personal loyalty and harmony are greatest at this level of the public service.[31] Even at the policy-

* This and the following question are reproduced from Robert O'Neil's *The Rights of Government Employees* (New York: Avon Books, 1978).

making level, however, a discharge that either violated a clear property interest or seriously jeopardized an employee's liberty might still require a hearing. The courts have never suggested that people who assume senior positions in the public service must completely abandon their constitutional rights.

If an internal procedure is provided by law, must a discharged employee pursue it before seeking external relief? *

In general, yes. Courts usually require that persons complaining of administrative action "exhaust" internal remedies before going outside the agency. There are sound reasons for this rule. The dispute may reflect a minor misunderstanding that can be quickly resolved even through an informal conference. Even where that is not possible, an internal procedure may sharpen the issues and possibly develop a record that will be useful at later stages. The time and expense in going outside the agency are obviously far greater, both for the individual employee and for the agency. And if everyone can bypass the internal procedures with impunity, they may cease to be meaningful even for those who wish to use them. Thus the exhaustion of internal remedies is usually required.

But there is an important exception: the remedy must be adequate to the grievant's needs. If an internal remedy would not have brought redress, then prior recourse to it may not always be required. In one recent federal case, a discharged fireman had gone directly to court, claiming that only a presuspension hearing would protect his constitutional rights. The court of appeals not only upheld the constitutional claim, but also agreed that he had properly bypassed the internal process because of its inadequacy. A 1976 Supreme Court decision allowed a disability-insurance claimant to bypass internal procedures because of compelling circumstances; the claimant had "raised a colorable claim that because of his physical condition and dependency upon the disability benefits, an erroneous termination would damage him in a way not recompensable through retroactive payments." [32] The claimant had also raised a basic constitutional claim, which was especially appropriate for resolution in the courts rather than

* See footnote to preceeding question.

in the very agency whose procedures were being questioned on constitutional grounds.

Such a course is risky, however. If a court later decides that the internal appeal is constitutionally adequate, the employee must then go back to the beginning, having lost substantial time (and probably money as well). Thus it is far wiser to pursue the internal procedures first, unless one is certain that bypassing them is justifiable.

NOTES

1. Board of Regents v. Roth, 408 U.S. 564, 577 (1972).
2. 426 U.S. 341, 344 (1976). See Swartout v. Civil Serv. Comm'n, 25 Wash. App. 174 (1980), petition for cert. filed, 49 U.S.L.W. 3010 (June 30, 1980) (No. 79–2078) (Washington public employees do not have property interest in public employment and name-clearing hearing is not required for suspension during probation).
3. Pierce v. Ortho Pharmaceutical Corp., 49 U.S.L.W. 2118 (N.J. July 28, 1980).
4. L. TRIBE, AMERICAN CONSTITUTIONAL LAW, §10–10, at 525 [hereinafter TRIBE].
5. 426 U.S. at 341 n. 13.
6. Id.
7. See Confederation of Police v. City of Chicago, 529 F.2d 89, 92 (7th Cir.), remanded, 427 U.S. 902 (1976), reversed on other grounds, 547 F.2d 375 (7th Cir. 1977) (affirming district court); Briggs v. City of Minneapolis, 358 F. Supp. 1340 (D. Minn. 1973).
8. Prosser, Privacy, 48 Calif. L. Rev. 383 (1960).
9. 426 U.S. 341 (1976); TRIBE, supra note 4, at 523.
10. 426 U.S. at 343.
11. Id. at 347.
12. Id. at 348.
13. 429 U.S. 624, 625 (1977). See Swartout v. Civil Serv. Comm'n, 25 Wash. App. 174 (1980), petition for cert. filed, 49 U.S.L.W. 3010 (June 30, 1980) (No. 79–2078) (Washington public employees do not have property interest in public employment and name-clearing hearing is not required for suspension during probation).
14. 429 U.S. at 626.
15. Id. at 628 (emphasis added).
16. Paul v. Davis, 424 U.S. 693 (1976).

17. *Id.* at 701. The Supreme Court said that its cases do not establish "the proposition that reputation alone, apart from some more tangible interest such as employment, is either 'liberty' or 'property' by itself sufficient to invoke the procedural protection of the Due Process Clause."

18. 429 U.S. at 628.

19. *Id.* at 627–28. *See also* Board of Regents v. Roth, 408 U.S. 564, 573 & n. 12 (1972) ("The purpose of such notice and hearing is to provide the person an opportunity to clear his name"). *See also* TRIBE, *supra* note 4, at 518.

20. 429 U.S. at 627.

21. 424 U.S. at 319, 334–35 (1976).

22. R. O'NEIL, THE RIGHTS OF GOVERNMENT EMPLOYEES 166 (1978).

23. 424 U.S. at 341.

24. *Cf.* Costa v. Board of Selectmen, 1979 Mass. Adv. Sh. 1088 (adequacy of notice under state statute).

25. *See* Vitarelli v. Seaton, 359 U.S. 535 (1959).

26. *Compare* Behan v. City of Dover, 419 F. Supp. 562 (D. Del. 1976), *aff'd mem.*, 559 F.2d 1207 (3d Cir. 1977).

27. Olshock v. Village of Skokie, 411 F. Supp. 257, 264 (N.D. Ill.), *aff'd* 541 F.2d 1254 (7th Cir. 1976).

28. Hortonville Joint School Dist. No. 1 v. Hortonville Educ. Ass'n., 426 U.S. 482 (1976).

29. Administrative Code of City of New York §434a–14.0(b) (1976).

30. Elrod v. Burns, 427 U.S. 347 (1976). *See also* Branti v. Finkel, 48 U.S.L.W. 4331 (U.S. Apr. 1, 1980).

31. Jaffree v. Scott, 372 F. Supp. 264 (N.D. Ill. 1974), *aff'd in past, rev'd in part, mem.*, 519 F.2d 1405 (7th Cir. 1975) (no property right, but remand regarding liberty interest in reputation), 590 F.2d 209 (7th Cir. 1978) (per curiam) (no liberty interest).

32. Mathews v. Eldridge, 424 U.S. 319 (1976).

VII

Use of Force

The use of deadly force by police officers has generated unparalleled controversy. Recent incidents of deaths caused by police officers in questionable circumstances have produced headlines in the media and outcries from the public, both criticizing and defending police practices.[1] Of perhaps greater ultimate significance, police administrators have recognized that officers need continuing education in the appropriate use of weapons.[2] Moreover, police departments have reevaluated departmental policy governing the circumstances in which use of weapons is justified. Indeed, the *New York Times* recently reported that, in the wake of three civilian deaths, the New York City Police Department would reconsider its policy on the use of deadly force by police officers, "particularly in dealing with violent emotionally disturbed people."[3]

The use of force by a police officer will be judged by three standards. The one with which most officers are most familiar is the compendium of rules and regulations of the police department. These rules are often stricter in limiting the use of force than corresponding state statutory or common law, the second source of guidelines for use of deadly force. The third source is constitutional law, both state and federal.

Because of the multiplicity of sources of an officer's authority to use force and because of the wide variety of legal standards, it is important for a police officer to be familiar with both departmental regulations and state law within his or her jurisdiction. The balance of this chapter treats questions related to the use of force in a general fashion, speaking in broad terms of how a number of police departments and states deal with the question.

Accordingly, it is essential, and this point cannot be emphasized strongly enough, that a police officer be thoroughly familiar with his or her department's guidelines for the use of deadly force. The general discussion herein should not be relied on, since this area of the police function is constantly subject to revised departmental requirements and changing state law. In addition, the appropriate use of deadly force may also be subject to evolving constitutional standards. If an officer has any doubts about the proper use of deadly force, he or she should consult with the department's lawyers.

What is deadly force?

Deadly force is that level of force which objectively would lead a reasonable police officer to conclude that its use "poses a high risk of death or serious injury to its human target, regardless of whether or not death, serious injury, or any harm actually results in a given case." [4] Firing a service revolver, using a nightstick on a subject's head, and running down a suspect with a police cruiser are examples of deadly force. Whether such force is permissible is of course a question separate from what level of force is deadly. Note that the definition speaks in objective terms. Whether an individual officer subjectively believed that use of the nightstick did not pose a high risk of death or serious injury is not determinative. The objective standard requires an evaluation of the level of force as seen through the eyes of the average reasonable police officer.

May deadly force be used to arrest a misdemeanor suspect?

Never.

At common law, a police officer could use deadly force to effect the arrest of one suspected of having committed any felony.[5] However, deadly force was not permitted to be used against a misdemeanor suspect.[6] Today, approximately twenty states continue to adhere to the common-law rule, either through statutes that have codified the common-law rule or through continued judicial adherence to the rule.[7] (In such states, however, local or departmental regulations may impose stricter limits on the use of deadly force.) A majority of states place greater restrictions on the use of deadly force than do common-law states, and of course, therefore, do not permit deadly force to arrest misdemeanor suspects.

Under the common-law rule, what crimes justify deadly force to effect an arrest?

Typically, at common law, the felonies justifying deadly force included murder, rape, manslaughter, robbery, sodomy, mayhem, burglary, arson, prison break, and larceny. Of course, this list of felonies, which dates approximately from the American Revolution, has expanded to include numerous other felonies, many of which do not involve force or danger to others. Now, in most jurisdictions, crimes such as bribery, embezzlement, kidnapping, and resisting arrest with force, to name only a few, are considered felonies and, therefore, would meet the simple definitional criterion for using deadly force in jurisdictions adhering to the common-law rule. Some states treat the commission of homosexual acts as a felony. However, it makes no sense to shoot a bribery suspect who runs away from an arresting officer or a homosexual for leaving the scene of a criminally defined homosexual encounter, since neither individual is likely to be a source of violent danger to the community and either can most likely be arrested at some other time.[8] Thus, in some instances, use of deadly force would be irrational, and indeed for that reason is unlikely to be used to arrest bribery suspects or homosexuals. Accordingly, a majority of states have modified the common-law rule and thus restricted the permissible scope for use of deadly force to forcible felonies only.

May a police officer fire warning shots before aiming at a fleeing suspect?

That depends upon the law in a given jurisdiction, which can vary markedly from one jurisdiction to another. Some departmental regulations, such as those of the Los Angeles County Sheriff's Department and the New York City Police Department,[9] prohibit the firing of warning shots altogether. The apparent rationale behind this prohibition is that the risk of warning shots to both the fleeing suspect and the innocent bystander is greater than the utility de-

rived from firing such warning shots. Similarly, numerous
police departments in the Los Angeles area, such as San
Marino, Montebello, and Palos Verdes Estates, forbid
warning shots to induce a suspect to surrender. The City
of Long Beach also forbids warning shots.[10]

The Missouri deadly-force statute, on the other hand,
requires only notice of intention to arrest the suspect before deadly force may be used. The statute does not specify
that the notice must be exclusively verbal, and thus arguably permits a warning shot.[11] Given the difference in
population density between New York City and at least
certain parts of the state of Missouri, the risks attendant
upon the firing of warning shots may be less. Admittedly,
warning shots that zing past three inches from the fleeing
suspect's ear would pose equivalent dangers to the suspect
in both areas. But outside of Missouri's major population
centers, the risks to bystanders would be reduced.

Remember that, even if a state does not forbid warning
shots, individual police departments still may.

Must a police officer warn a suspect verbally before using deadly force?

Under the majority rule and common law, a verbal
warning is not required. However, as a matter of practice,
a verbal warning is almost always given.[12]

How do states with deadly-force rules stricter than the common-law rule limit the use of deadly force?

A number of states—including Georgia, Illinois, New
York, North Dakota, Oregon, Pennsylvania, and Utah—
either specify certain felonies that may justify deadly force
or require that only forcible felonies may justify deadly
force.[13] A number of other states—including Delaware,
Hawaii, Kentucky, Maine, Nebraska, North Carolina, and
Texas—have substantially followed the approach of the
Model Penal Code.[14] Under the Model Code, the arresting
officer must believe that the suspect committed a felony
(1) which "involved conduct including the use or threatened use of force" or (2) which leads the arresting officer
to conclude that there is a "substantial risk that the person
to be arrested will cause death or serious bodily harm if
his apprehension is delayed." [15] Thus, the president of a
corporation charged with a white-collar crime could not

be arrested with the use of deadly force, should force be necessary to effect his arrest. A more common eventuality arises in the case of car theft. Under the state laws of the states listed above and of other states adhering to the rule limiting deadly force to arrests for violent felonies only, garden-variety car thefts would not justify the use of deadly force. By contrast, car thefts justify such force under the common-law rule in those jurisdictions where car theft is a felony.

Must the police officer witness the felony to use deadly force?

Not under the common-law rule. Once the officer has probable cause to make an arrest of a suspected felon, the officer may use deadly force to arrest the felony suspect.[16]

However, not all jurisdictions are in agreement. For example, Boston police officers may shoot a fleeing felon only where the officer *"knows, as a virtual certainty, . . .* that the subject has committed a felony during the commission of which he inflicted or threatened to inflict deadly force upon the victim, and . . . that there is substantial risk that the felon in question will cause death or great bodily injury if his apprehension is delayed."[17] Clearly, the Boston rule is stringent. The "virtual-certainty" standard is not only stricter than the "probable-cause" standard, but also stricter than the usual criminal proof standard of "beyond a reasonable doubt." The practical effect of the rule then, except in very rare circumstances, is to require the police officer to witness the felony in order to be permitted to shoot at the felon in flight. Otherwise the officer utilizes deadly force at his or her peril.

By contrast, former regulations of the Los Angeles County Sheriff's Department, although ambiguous, appeared on their face to permit use of deadly force to effect felony arrests where the officer had "reasonable cause determined from credible or observed acts that a felony has been committed."[18] Thus a statement by a "credible" witness that someone had just committed a felony would have justified the use of deadly force to effect an arrest for that felony. The literal Los Angeles County standard formerly in effect was substantially identical to the common-law "probable-cause" standard.

Must a police officer, who is otherwise justified in using deadly force, refrain where there are bystanders present?

Often. New York City Police Department regulations, for example, require police officers to refrain from discharging firearms if innocent persons may be endangered. Similarly, the Model Penal Code proscribes deadly force unless "the actor believes that the force employed creates no substantial risk of injury to innocent persons." [19] And in Massachusetts, the Supreme Judicial Court recently ruled that police officers may discharge firearms only when they believe there is no reasonable danger to innocent bystanders.[20] Thus, whether the presence of bystanders will require police officers to refrain from using deadly force will depend on the particular facts or circumstances of an event, such as whether the bystanders are in or near the line of fire.

By contrast, many common-law states do not prohibit use of deadly force in the presence of bystanders. This rule of state law is often tempered, however, by individual police departments that prohibit the use of deadly force where bystanders may be endangered.

Do police departments often adopt stricter rules on use of deadly force than the minimum requirements under state law?

Yes. In 1974, for example, the Boston Police Department adopted internal Rule 303, which permits an officer to discharge a firearm "To defend himself or another [person] from an unlawful attack which he has reasonable cause to believe could result in death or great bodily injury" or "To apprehend a fleeing felon when the officer knows, as a virtual certainty, . . . that the subject has committed a felony during the commission of which he inflicted or threatened to inflict deadly force upon the victim, and . . . that there is substantial risk that the felon in question will cause death or great bodily injury if his apprehension is delayed." [21] The rule sharply limits the instances under which a Boston police officer may use deadly force. Deadly force in self-defense is justified in Boston only where the attacker is himself using deadly force. Deadly force against fleeing felons is also strictly circumscribed: the officer must know to a virtual certainty that a felony was committed, that the victim suffered or was threatened with deadly force, and that the threat of violence is likely to recur. Thus, a simple burglary, for example, would not permit a Boston police officer to use deadly force.

The Los Angeles County Sheriff's Department now apparently restricts use of deadly force to life-threatening situations.[22] The motivation for absolute adherence to this stricter policy has been enhanced recently by the California Supreme Court's decision in *Peterson* v. *City of Long Beach*, which held that violation of a departmental regulation governing use of firearms raised a presumption of negligence on the part of the officer even though the use of deadly force may have been permissible under state law. [23] The practical effect of such a presumption is to make a potential plaintiff's burden of proving negligence easier. Moreover, the officer would not be able to defend his or her actions by claiming that state law permitted the level of force actually used.

Other police departments have, at various times, adopted limitations similar to those embodied in the Model Penal Code. These include Kansas City, Missouri; Knoxville, Tennessee; Charlotte, North Carolina; Washington, D.C.; Oakland, California; and New Haven, Connecticut, among others.[24] Since 1977, officers of the Los Angeles Police Department have been allowed to use deadly force to apprehend a fleeing felon only where a "crime involving serious bodily injury or use of deadly force" has been committed and "where there is a substantial risk that the person whose arrest is sought will cause death or serious bodily injury to others if apprehension is delayed." [25]

Is the federal rule different from the majority state rule?
Yes. Federal law-enforcement officers are not permitted to use deadly force except in self-defense or to protect the lives of threatened persons.[26]

Are there circumstances other than arrest where deadly force may be used?
Yes. Deadly force may also be permitted in self-defense, to counter violent resistance to an arrest, to prevent the commission of a crime, to prevent escape or to recapture after escape from arrest or from a penal institution, and

to stop a riot. Of course, the circumstances under which deadly force may be used vary from state to state.

Most jurisdictions and the Model Penal Code authorize use of deadly force to prevent crimes which endanger life or threaten serious bodily harm.[27] New York City officers, for example, may use firearms to defend themselves or others from the application of force, but department regulations caution officers to use the minimum amount of force needed to accomplish the mission.[28] Personnel of the Los Angeles County Sheriff's Department "have the positive duty to use firearms whenever the necessity exists in the protection of their lives, or the lives of others." [29]

In cases where a suspect resists an arrest through use of violent force, a police officer may ordinarily use the level of force permitted by the state self-defense statute unless departmental regulations are more stringent. Ordinarily, a police officer "has the right to use the force which is reasonably necessary to overcome resistance by the person sought to be arrested." [30] The context in which the application of force occurs will have a bearing on its reasonableness. For example, the Commonwealth of Massachusetts explicitly recognizes the authority of prison guards, because of the nature of the job, "to apply force to inmates where necessary to preserve order in the institution." [31] The level of force permitted is that which is reasonable under all of the circumstances.[32] Thus, the prison context, the manner by which force was initiated, whether weapons were involved, and the physical capabilities of the prisoners would all presumably be relevant factors.

Where an arrested person attempts to escape from custody, the Model Penal Code allows that level of force to prevent the escape which could have been employed to effect the arrest pursuant to which the person is in custody. Thus, a person arrested for a misdemeanor could not have his attempted escape from arrest prevented by deadly force pursuant to the Model Penal Code. However, in states which provide that such an escape is, in and of itself, a felony and which adhere to the common-law deadly-force rule permitting deadly force to arrest putative felons, presumably deadly force could be used to prevent the escape from custody of such misdemeanants. Even under the Model Penal Code, deadly force is permissible where the escaping person is attempting to escape from a jail, prison, or other institution for the detention of persons charged with or convicted of a crime. Thus, whether one attempts to escape from a police car or a jail can determine the level of force that peace officers may use.

Finally, a number of states allow deadly force to be used to stop a riot.[33]

Are deadly-force statutes constitutional?

Some probably are but some may not be. Statutes embodying the common-law rule seem most susceptible to constitutional challenge. Indeed such challenges have been brought, in which plaintiffs have claimed that deadly-force statutes embodying the common-law rule violate the due-process and equal-protection clauses of the Fourteenth Amendment and the Eighth Amendment's prohibition against cruel and unusual punishment.[34]

In *Mattis* v. *Schnarr,* for example, eighteen-year-old Michael Mattis was killed by a police officer after being discovered with a friend in the office of a golf driving range at 1:20 A.M.[35] When the officer ordered him to halt, Michael fled and was shot to death.[36] The Missouri statute, pursuant to which the police officer fired, provided for the use of deadly force in attempting to apprehend any person for any felony. The statute required the arresting police officer to give notice of his intent to arrest the suspect. Upon either flight or forcible resistance by the suspect, deadly force was then permissible.

The federal district court validated the statute, but the United States Court of Appeals for the Eighth Circuit reversed, ruling the statute unconstitutional. The circuit court found that the statute violated the due-process guarantee because the level of procedural protection accorded Mattis—observation of a break-in and a verbal warning to halt—was insufficient to justify the taking of his liberty and his life. The process was deficient because there was no reasonable relationship between the use of deadly force and the legitimate exercise of the police power, since that exercise must be directed at protecting the police or others from bodily harm. Because there was no rational relationship between the statute and legitimate state objectives, the law violated the due-process clause.

The Supreme Court subsequently vacated the Eighth Circuit's decision on the ground that the plaintiff had no present right at stake and that accordingly no case or controversy existed. In the Court of Appeals, the plaintiff (the decedent's father) only requested declaratory and injunctive relief, that is, a ruling that the Missouri law is unconstitutional and that its further application is prohibited. Because this relief could not help the plaintiff even if granted, there was no ongoing case or controversy. Presumably, if the father had claimed money damages, the Eighth Circuit could have properly decided the law's constitutionality. Nevertheless, the opinion remains a strong statement about the Missouri law's unconstitutionality should the statute be properly challenged in the future.

Of course, courts in other jurisdictions have upheld the constitutionality of deadly-force statutes similar to that criticized by the Eighth Circuit.[37] Still, the Eighth Circuit's reasoning seems persuasive. Ultimately, the Supreme Court will likely have to resolve the dispute.

Statutes and regulations that embody the requirements of the Model Penal Code are more likely to be upheld as constitutional. Because the use of deadly force is limited to instances where it is necessary to protect human life and safety or where a violent felony has been committed, there is a rational connection between the force authorized by the statute or regulations and the legitimate state objectives sought to be advanced by the statute or regulations. Clearly, police protection of the lives and safety of others and themselves is a proper objective; the use of deadly force in such instances or when a violent felony has been committed may be adequately tailored to advance the legitimate governmental objectives implicated.

Might police officers be held liable for use of deadly force pursuant to the common-law rule under Section 1983?

Yes. If indeed the deadly-force statute is unconstitutional and an individual is deprived of his or her life pursuant to force authorized by the statute, a police officer might be sued for constitutional deprivation under Section 1983 of Title 42 of the United States Code. The officer would of course have a limited "good faith" defense which may immunize him or her from a damage claim [38] if the officer acted in "objective" and "subjective" good faith.[39]

Good faith would be lacking, however, if "the constitutional right allegedly infringed . . . was clearly established at the time of [the] challenged conduct, if [he or she] knew or should have known of that right, and if [he or she] knew or should have known that [the] conduct violated the constitutional norm." [40] (See Chapter VIII for a fuller discussion of police officers' potential liabilities.)

At this point in most parts of the country, it is difficult to conclude that the constitutional right of a suspect to be free of excessive force in nondangerous situations is clearly established. However, the Eighth Circuit has spoken *en banc;* and even though the decision was ultimately vacated by the Supreme Court, it is essential that police officers and departments within the Eighth Circuit act with the greatest caution in using deadly force. To follow the letter of state law may not adequately protect them from liability. There appears to be no other circuit court opinion which has spoken so unambiguously. Nevertheless, if and when courts begin to strike down the common-law use of deadly force, police officers and departments must be attentive to such developments in order to protect against possible liability for the use of deadly force which is authorized by state statute or departmental regulation but which may nevertheless be unconstitutional.

In addition to civil damages liability in federal court for violation of constitutional rights, are there other sanctions which may be imposed on police officers for improper use of force?

Yes. Police officers may be subject to state criminal prosecution where they have improperly used deadly force. In New York City, a local grand jury is empanelled each time deadly force is used to determine if its use was appropriate. The federal government also has prosecutorial power against intentional violations of federal constitutional rights from, for example, excessive use of force. State damages actions may also be brought by the victim of excessive force, or the representative of an estate, under traditional tort law theories of assault, battery and negligence. In the case of negligence, police departments may also be liable in some jurisdictions for the negligent acts of their officers. (This subject is explored more fully in

Chapter VIII.) Finally, police departments may discipline their officers who have violated departmental guidelines on the use of deadly force.

NOTES

1. N.Y. Times, Sept. 9, 1979, §4, at 6E, cols. 1–4.
2. Dorfman, *Deadly Force* 6 Barrister (No. 1) 15, 54 (1979) [hereinafter Dorfman].
2. *See* N.Y. Times, Sept. 9. 1979, §4 at 6E, col. 1.
4. Comment, *Deadly Force to Arrest: Triggering Constitutional Review,* 11 Harv. C.R-C.L.L. Rev. 361, 363 (1976) (footnote omitted) [hereinafter Comment, *Deadly Force*].
5. *E.g.,* Stinnett v. Virginia, 55 F.2d 644 (4th Cir. 1932); *see* Comment, *Deadly Force, supra* note 4, at 364 and n. 13.
6. E.g., Thomas v. Kinkead, 55 Ark. 502, 18 S.W. 854 (1892); *See* Comment, *Deadly Force, supra* note 4, at 365 & n. 13.
7. Winter, *Deadly Force Laws Under Fire After Miami,* 66 A.B.A.J. 828 (1980); *see* Comment, *Deadly Force, supra* note 4, at 368–69. *See also* Sherman, *Perspectives on Police and Violence,* 452 Annals of the American Academy of Political and Social Science 10 (Nov. 1980); Sherman, *Execution Without Trial: Police Homicide and the Constitution,* 33 Vand. L. Rev. 71, 71–72 (1980).
8. Comment, *Deadly Force, supra* note 4, at 365–66; Manning, *Violence and the Police Role,* 452 Annals of the American Academy of Political and Social Science 141 (Nov. 1980).
9. Policy and Ethics of the Los Angeles County Sheriff's Department, §3–01/030.30 (1979); New York City Patrol Guide (General Regulations) 6 (1976).
10. *See* Long Beach Police Officers Ass'n v. City of Long Beach, 61 Cal. App. 3d 364, 132 Cal. Rptr. 348 (1976).
11. *See* V.A.M.S. §544.190.
12. Telephone interview with Kenneth Conboy, Deputy Commissioner, New York City Police Department (Apr. 4, 1980).
13. *See* Comment, *Deadly Force, supra* note 4, at 368 & n. 31, *citing* Ga. Code Ann. §26–902; Ill. Rev. Stat. ch. 38, §7–5(A)(2); N.Y. Penal Law §35–30(1)(a)(ii); N.D. Cent. Code §12.1–05–07(2)(d); Ore. Rev. State. §161.239.

Pa. Stat. Ann. tit. 18, §508(a)(1)(ii); Utah Code Ann. §76–2–404(2)(b).

14. *See id,* at 368–69 & n. 32, *citing* Del. Code Ann. tit. 11, §467(c); Haw. Rev. Stat. §703–307(3); Ky. Rev. Stat. §503.90(2); Me. Rev. Stat. Ann. tit. 17A §107(2); Neb. Rev. Stat. §28–839(3); N.C. Gen. Stat. §15a–401(d)(2) (b); Tex. Penal Code Ann. §9.51(c).

15. Model Penal Code §§3.04–3.11 (Proposed official Draft, 1962).

16. *See, e.g.,* Commonwealth v. Snow, 363 Mass. 778, 788 (1973).

17. Boston Police Department Rule 303 (emphasis added), *quoted in* Reinstein v. Commissioner, No. S-1714, Slip op. at 3, (Mass. Sup. Jud. Ct. June 19, 1979).

18. Uelmen, *Varieties of Police Behavior: A Study of Police Policy Regarding the Use of Deadly Force in Los Angeles County,* 6 Loy. L.A.L. Rev. 1, 27 (1973).

19. Model Penal Code, §3.07(2)(b).

20. Julian v. Randazzo, 1980 Mass. Adv. Sh. 965, 970 & n. 1.

21. Rule 303, *quoted in* Reinstein v. Commissioner, No. S-1714, Slip op. at 3, (Mass. Sup. Jud. Ct., June 20, 1979).

22. Policy and Ethics of Los Angeles County Sheriff's Department, §3–01/030.30 (1979); telephone interview with Sergeant Foster of Legal Section of Los Angeles County Sheriff's Office (June 4, 1980).

23. Peterson v. City of Long Beach, 24 Cal. 3d 238, 155 Cal. Rptr. 360, 594 P.2d 477 (1979).

24. *See* Comment, *Deadly Force, supra* note 4, at 370 & n. 42.

25. Meyer, *"Statistical Analysis of Los Angeles Police Department Officer Involved Shootings, 1974–1978/79,"* quoted in Reiss, *Police Use of Deadly Force,* 452 *Annals of the American Academy of Political and Social Science* 126 (Nov. 1980).

26. *See* Dorfman, *supra note 2,* at 54; Sherman, *supra,* note 7, at 92.

27. *See* Comment, *Deadly Force, supra* note 4, at 361 n. 2.

28. New York City Patrol Guide (General Regulations) 6 (1976).

29. Policy and Ethics of Los Angeles County Sheriff's Department, §3–01/030.30 (1979).

30. J. Nolan, 32 Massachusetts Practice (Criminal Law) §652, at 485 (1976).

31. Commonwealth v. Martin, 369 Mass. 640, 341 N.E.2d 885, 891–92 (1976).

32. *Cf.* Commonwealth v. Shaffer, 367 Mass. 508, 326 N.E.2d 880 (1975).

33. Comment, *Deadly Force, supra* note 4, at 361 n. 2.

34. *E.g.,* Mattis v. Schnarr, 404 F. Supp. 643 (E.D. Mo. 1975), *rev'd,* 547 F.2d 1007 (8th Cir. 1976) (en banc), *vacated sub. nom.* Ashcroft v. Mattis, 431 U.S. 171 (1977) (per curiam); *see* Wolfer v. Thaler, 525 F.2d 977 (5th Cir.), *cert. denied,* 425 U.S. 975 (1976); Jones v. Marshall, 528 F.2d 132 (2d Cir. 1975).

35. 404 F. Supp. 643 (E.D. Mo. 1975).

36. *Id.* at 644.

37. *E.g.,* Wiley v. Memphis Police Dep't, 548 F.2d 1247 (6th Cir.), *cert. denied,* 434 U.S. 822 (1977); Jones v. Marshall, 528 F.2d 132 (2d Cir. 1975).

38. *See* Procunier v. Navarette, 434 U.S. 555 (1978); Wood v. Strickland, 420 U.S. 308 (1975).

39. *Id.* at 321–22.

40. Procunier v. Navarette, 434 U.S. at 562.

VIII

The Officer in Court

In our litigation-minded society, plaintiffs and defendants, both, should be aware of their respective rights and liabilities. This chapter explores issues of concern to the police officer who is sued—or who sues a superior or the department—in a civil action. It treats questions of liability, immunity, indemnity, and damages. Civil suits brought by police officers against citizens are treated in Chapter IX.

Can a police officer be sued?

Yes. Unlike kings, judges, and prosecutors, police officers can be sued for their official acts.[1] Courts have unanimously refused to grant police officers an absolute immunity from lawsuits that challenge acts committed within the scope of their employment and seek the remedy of damages.[2] Rather they are afforded a *qualified* immunity: they are exempt from liability for actions taken in good faith *and* with the reasonable belief that the action is lawful.[3]

Can a police department, town or city be sued for the wrongful acts of its police employees?

Yes, depending upon the circumstances.

Earlier in our nation's history, and still today in some states, a state or municipality could not be sued under any circumstances for damages arising from the common-law negligence of its employees.[4] Sovereign immunity derived from the notion that the "King can do no wrong," a concept that finds little acceptance in a modern democracy.[5] Thus courts and legislatures have in large part modified or abolished the doctrine.[6] A statute of the State of New York, for example, provides that "every city, county, town, village, authority or agency shall be liable for . . . any negligent act or tort," provided that the duly appointed police officer charged with committing the act "was acting in the performance of his duties and within the scope of his employment."[7] Similarly, by virtue of the Federal Tort Claims Act, the federal government has waived immunity for many tortious acts of its employees.[8] In all jurisdictions, the localities may be liable under specified conditions for the constitutional infractions of their employees.

Not every act by a subordinate gives rise to governmental liability, however. Nor does every act trigger personal liability for the official. Although the original rationale for sovereign immunity may be outmoded, "the common law soon recognized the necessity for permitting officials to perform their official functions free from the threat of suits for personal liability."[9] Two modern rationales, therefore, support the doctrine of the limited immunity of public officials:

1. It would be unjust to hold an officer personally liable when he or she acts in good faith and is legally obliged to make choices and judgments.
2. The threat of such liability would make the officer unwilling to do the job with the decisiveness and the judgment required by the public good.[10]

The circumstances under which public officials and governments are liable in court are treated later in this chapter.

What are the bases for the liability of a police officer or department?

The two principal bases are (1) common-law torts such as assault, battery, and false imprisonment, and (2) Section 1983 of Title 42 of the United States Code. Section 1983 provides that:

Every person who, under color of any statute, ordinance, regulation, custom, or usage, of any State or Territory, subjects, or causes to be subjected, any citizen of the United States or other person within

the jurisdiction thereof to the deprivation of any
rights, privileges, or immunities secured by the Constitution and laws, shall be liable to the party injured
in an action at law, suit in equity, or other proper
proceeding for redress.[11]

What must be proven in a lawsuit under Section 1983?

To prevail in a Section 1983 action, a plaintiff must
establish (1) that the defendant deprived the plaintiff of
a right secured under the federal laws or Constitution,
and (2) that the defendant was acting "under color of
state law." [12] The first element of a Section 1983 violation
—federal constitutional or statutory deprivation—can occur where an officer recklessly shoots and kills a suspect
or a bystander, since the victim is deprived of the right to
life guaranteed under the Fourteenth Amendment.[13] A
second example is a forcible entry into a person's home
without a warrant or in the absence of exigent circumstances, a violation of the Fourth and Fourteenth Amendments' guarantees against unreasonable searches and
seizures.[14] A Section 1983 claim is frequently triggered by
a constitutional violation, and is therefore often called a
"constitutional tort."

The second ingredient of a Section 1983 claim—the
defendant acting "under color of state law, custom or
usage"—requires both that the defendant act "under state
color" and that the conduct constitute "state action." [15]
These two concepts often blur, and are satisfied when a
police officer—a public employee—acts in an official capacity. It is also clear that these two tests are not met
when an officer acts purely in a personal capacity. Someone who falls on the steps of an officer's home cannot
sue for damages under Section 1983, since the officer's
housekeeping was not clothed with the authority of the
state. (The injured party could, of course, sue the officer
under common-law negligence.) More problematic is the
situation where an off-duty officer shoots a victim. Is such
a quasi-official or unofficial act taken "under color of
state law"? In *Belcher* v. *Stengel,* the Supreme Court decided not to decide this important issue, and thus left
standing the lower-court award of damages against an
off-duty officer who killed two people and disabled a third
in a barroom brawl.[16] A standard that may be applied in

determining "color" is that the officer misused power that was "possessed by virtue of state law and made possible only because the wrongdoer is clothed with the authority of state law." [17]

Can federal officers be sued under Section 1983?

No. Federal officers do not act under "color of state" law; thus their conduct is not regulated by Section 1983.[18] Rather, federal officers can be sued directly for their constitutional infractions in what is called a "Bivens action." Although Section 1983, as originally enacted, did not cover police officers of the District of Columbia,[19] a recent amendment extended the statute to reach official conduct in the nation's capital.[20] The liability of federal officers is discussed later in this chapter.

Can state tort law be used to hold police liable for their misconduct?

Yes. A common source of police officers' liability is state tort law. An officer may be liable in tort where the officer unreasonably caused injury to the plaintiff or exposed the plaintiff to an unreasonable risk of harm.[21] An officer can commit a state tort whether or not the act in question violated the Constitution or a federal statute. Examples of common-law torts are assault, battery, false imprisonment, and negligence.

Although state laws differ, an *assault* is usually defined as one person causing another reasonably to fear that he or she will suffer immediate injury.[22] For example, an officer points a loaded gun at a bystander. Damages are recoverable just because of the plaintiff's apprehension, even if no physical injuries ensue. A *battery* may occur when an officer inflicts injury on another, through unconsented physical contact.[23] An officer commits *false imprisonment* (sometimes called false arrest) when the victim is unlawfully restrained or detained within a bounded or defined area.[24] *Negligence* is a catch-all tort, and can occur whenever the following four elements are established: (1) a duty on the part of the officer or department to act with care toward the plaintiff, (2) a breach of the duty, (3) damages to the plaintiff, and (4) a direct link between the breach of duty and the harm suffered.[25]

What is an example of a negligence action?

In *McCrink* v. *City of New York,* a police officer, off-duty and concededly intoxicated, shot and killed Francis McCrink and seriously wounded another.[26] The assault was unprovoked. Four months after the shooting, the officer was diagnosed as a psychotic due to alcohol, and civilly committed as insane. Over a period of years prior to the shooting, the officer had been subject to three disciplinary proceedings based on intoxication. McCrink's estate and the wounded victim sued the City of New York for damages. The New York Court of Appeals ruled that where the department's retention of the police officer involved a *foreseeable* risk of bodily harm to others (including the public), its retention was negligent, and the city could be held liable for the resultant death of McCrink and injury to another. Interestingly, a federal district court has also held that "where a city's failure to train, supervise or discipline police officers is reckless or grossly negligent, it may . . . serve as a basis for holding a city liable under Section 1983." [27]

What are other sources of protection for victims of police misconduct?

In addition to Section 1983 and state tort law, miscellaneous federal and state laws provide redress to victims of police misconduct.[28] In 1979, for example, Massachusetts enacted a civil-rights statute similar to Section 1983.[29] The Massachusetts law is broader, though, because it dispenses with the "color of state law" requirement, and appears to grant relief whenever an individual's constitutional or statutory rights are violated.

Does Section 1983 provide redress for all improper police conduct?

No. A Section 1983 violation requires breach of a federal right, either constitutional or statutory.[30] The U.S. Supreme Court has not directly confronted the question whether negligent police conduct can amount to a constitutional infraction.[31] Where negligent conduct has been before the court, it decided—for other reasons—that such conduct was not remediable under Section 1983. In *Paul* v. *Davis,* for example, the Court held that the police department's circulation of a flyer labeling the plaintiff as an "active shoplifter" and potentially injuring his reputation, did not amount to a constitutional violation.[32] In *Estelle* v. *Gamble*, the Court held that the negligent failure to provide medical care to prisoners was a state tort and not a constitutional violation, but noted that an intentional or grossly negligent withholding would be unconstitutional.[33] In *Baker* v. *McCollan*, the Court held that the negligent detention of the wrong person pursuant to a warrant did not violate Section 1983.[34] As one federal district court explained, "Where only simple negligence is involved, the central focus of Section 1983, abuse of official power or position, is not implicated." [35] In *Parratt* v. *Taylor*, the Supreme Court agreed to review the issue whether simple negligence, if proven, may form the basis of a Section 1983 judgment.[36]

Does Section 1983 always require that misconduct be "willful"?

No. Although the courts are divided as to whether merely negligent conduct can give rise to a Section 1983 violation,[37] the Supreme Court [38] and the lower courts [39] have ruled that reckless or grossly negligent acts may give rise to a Section 1983 violation.

Are defenses available to a police officer who is sued under Section 1983?

Yes. In *Pierson* v. *Ray*, the Supreme Court recognized that an officer's good faith *and* reasonable belief that his or her conduct was lawful would constitute a defense to an action for damages under Section 1983.[40] In *Wood* v. *Strickland*, the Court elaborated upon the "good faith" defense:

> As we see it, the appropriate standard [of good faith] necessarily contains elements of both ["subjective" and "objective" factors]. The official must himself be acting sincerely and with a belief that he is doing right. . . . [Additionally the official] must be held to a standard of conduct based not only on permissible intentions, but also on knowledge of the basic, unquestioned constitutional rights of his charges. . . .[41]

Succinctly stated, evidence must demonstrate not only that the officer "believed, in good faith, that his conduct was lawful, but also that his belief was reasonable." [42] The officer's reasonable and good-faith belief may be based on state or local law, the advice of counsel, administrative practice, and other reasonable factors.[43] Good faith would be lacking, for example, if "the constitutional right allegedly infringed . . . was clearly established at the time of [the] challenged conduct, if [the officer] knew or should have known of the right, and if [he or she] knew or should have known that [the] conduct violated the constitutional norm." [44]

Is acting in good faith a defense available to officers in common-law tort actions?

Yes, in most instances. The good-faith and reasonable-belief defense is available to officers in cases of false arrest and imprisonment and wrongful arrest, entry,[45] but not always in assault and battery.[46] Additionally, administrative and higher-level police officials are ordinarily immune from federal and state tort suits if their acts are "discretionary" policy judgments, as contrasted with "ministerial" tasks. The District of Columbia Court of Appeals explained: "Discretionary functions are activities of such a nature as to pose threats to the quality and efficiency of government . . . if liability in tort were made the consequence of negligent acts or omissions. Thus, to prevent a stalemate in policy choices and decision-making, government bodies are immune from [state tort] suits aimed at the results of those decisions." [47]

Can a state fashion its own tort-immunity law and grant a municipality and its officials absolute immunity from state tort actions?

Yes. In *Martinez* v. *California*, decided in January 1980, the Supreme Court upheld the constitutionality of a California statute that absolutely immunized parole officials from state tort actions. Plaintiffs charged that the statute violated the due-process clause. The Court disagreed and explained that

the State's interest in fashioning its own rules of tort law is paramount to any discernible federal interest, [unless the immunity grant] is wholly arbitrary or irrational. . . . [Here however] there "is a rational relationship between the State's purpose and the statute." . . . [T]he California Legislature could reasonably conclude that judicial review of a parole officer's decision "would inevitably inhibit the exercise of discretion." . . . That inhibiting effect could impair the State's ability to implement a parole program. . . . Whether one agrees or disagrees with California's decision to provide absolute immunity for parole officials . . . , it rationally furthers a policy that reasonable lawmakers may favor.[48]

May states broaden, modify, or abolish the qualified immunity accorded police officers in Section 1983 actions?
No. The scope and availability of Section 1983 immunity and its defenses are questions of federal law,[49] and cannot be enlarged, lessened, or otherwise modified by state courts or legislatures.[50] As discussed above, states can alter immunities and remedies available under state tort law.

Who bears the burden of pleading and proving that the police officer acted in "good faith" and with "reasonable belief"?
In *Gomez* v. *Toledo*,[51] decided in May 1980, the Supreme Court unanimously ruled that in Section 1983 actions, the burden rests with the defendant to plead the good-faith defense. Thus a plaintiff states a claim under Section 1983 by alleging violation of a federal right and action under color of state law; the plaintiff need not additionally allege in the complaint that the defendant acted in bad faith. Rather, the officer who invokes the good-faith defense must raise it in the officer's answer to the plaintiff's complaint.

This allocation of the burden of pleading is logical, since the elements constituting the good-faith defense (that is, the reasonable and subjective belief that the officer's conduct was lawful) lie within the peculiar knowledge and control of the defendant.[52] For similar reasons, the burden of *proving* the good faith defense probably also rests with the defendant officer,[53] although in *Gomez* the Supreme Court did not expressly decide the question of the burden of proof.[54]

In common-law false-imprisonment actions, the police officer is required to allege and prove the good-faith defense.[55]

Can an officer invoke the good-faith defense in actions that do not request money damages?

No. The good-faith defense (or, as it is often called, qualified immunity) applies only in lawsuits seeking money damages.[56] It does not apply in actions for declaratory or injunctive relief,[57] or in criminal proceedings. In a declaratory action, the plaintiff seeks merely a declaration by the court that certain action is lawful or unlawful. In an injunctive action, the plaintiff asks the court to prevent or compel future conduct, not to remedy past injury through a damage award. Courts have reasoned that in these contexts, where plaintiffs seek only to restrain future unlawful conduct, there is no reason to immunize an official from suit.[58]

More problematic is whether immunity applies when a plaintiff requests the remedy of back pay. This situation might arise where an officer sues a superior and alleges an unconstitutional discharge. Although back pay appears functionally similar to an award of damages to compensate for past misconduct, courts have traditionally not labeled back pay as compensatory.[59] Thus, it is unclear whether the immunity that traditionally attaches to damage awards also attaches to requests for back pay.[60]

May a police department or locality be sued under Section 1983?

Yes. Until 1978, the Supreme Court had conferred on localities an absolute immunity from Section 1983 lawsuits.[61] The basis for the immunity was the Court's reading of Congress's intention in 1871 (when it first enacted the provision) that municipalities be exempt from its reach. In 1978 in *Monell* v. *Department of Social Services*, though, the Supreme Court exhaustively canvassed the legislative history of the statute and overruled its earlier reading.[62] Justice Brennan explained that Congress *did* intend that, in proper circumstances, municipalities and other local government units be accountable to Section 1983 plaintiffs.

In what circumstances are localities liable under Section 1983?

Local governing bodies . . . can be directly sued under §1983 for monetary. declaratory. or injunctive relief where . . . the action that is alleged to be unconstitutional implements or executes a policy statement, ordinance, regulation, or decision officially adopted and promulgated by that body's officers. Moreover, although the touchstone of the §1983 action against a government body is an allegation that official policy is responsible for a deprivation of rights protected by the Constitution, local governments. like every other §1983 "person," by the very terms of the statute, may be sued for constitutional deprivations visited. pursuant to governmental "custom" even though such a custom has not received formal approval through the body's official decision-making channels. . . . "Congress included custom and usages [in §1983] because of the persistent and widespread discriminatory practices of state officials. . . . Although not authorized by written law, such practices of state officials could well be so permanent and well settled as to constitute a 'custom or usage' with the force of law."

On the other hand, the language of §1983, read against the background of the same legislative history, compels the conclusion that Congress did not intend municipalities to be held liable unless action pursuant to official municipal policy of some nature caused a constitutional tort. In particular, . . . a municipality cannot be held liable *solely* because it employs a [person who commits a tort]—or, in other words, a municipality cannot be held liable under §1983 on a [strict liability] theory.[63]

Thus, the circumstances that render cities liable under Section 1983 differ from those imposing liability under state tort law. Cities are liable under Section 1983 when an official municipal policy or ingrained local custom causes a constitutional deprivation. Under state tort law, and only in jurisdictions that have waived sovereign immunity, a locality is generally liable for the negligence of an employee unless the wrongdoing resulted from a "discretionary" policy judgment.[64] In short, cities may be liable for high-level misconduct under Section 1983 and for low-level misconduct under state tort law.

The case of *Chandler* v. *District of Columbia* starkly portrays the distinction.[65] There the fire department maintained a program of closing fire stations on a rotating basis. A mother who lost two children in a fire that occurred near a closed station sued the government in tort. The court concluded that the rotating closure program was a discretionary government action; thus the doctrine of sovereign immunity prevented recovery. Since the station-closure program was in all likelihood an official policy, however, the municipality would have been liable under Section 1983 if it had committed a constitutional deprivation. There is another hitch, however: the District of Columbia, the defendant in the lawsuit, was not liable under Section 1983 until after the suit was filed. But when Section 1983 applies, the common-law defense used in *Chandler* is unavailable. As the Supreme Court recently explained: "a municipality has no 'discretion' to violate the Federal Constitution; its dictates are absolute and imperative." [66]

What sort of "official" city "policy" gives rise to municipal liability under Section 1983?

The law is evolving that (1) a departmental regulation or program, (2) a decision by high departmental officials, and (3) conduct by high officials evincing implicit approval or acquiescence in a pattern (or possibly incident) of behavior by subordinates each constitutes an "official policy" for purposes of Section 1983.[67]

Take as an example the city's behavior in *Owen* v. *City of Independence*, a case decided by the Supreme Court in April 1980.[68] *Owen* arose from the city's discharge of its police chief. The city manager and city council had grown increasingly dissatisfied with Owen's performance. At a formal meeting, the city council charged the chief with incompetence and directed the manager to take "appropriate action" under the city charter. The city charter empowered the manager to discharge department heads without notice or a hearing. Welcoming the cue from the council, the manager fired Owen. Owen's subsequent request for a hearing was denied. The Eighth Circuit Court of Appeals concluded that the manager's and council's actions amounted to official policy because Owen's firing was based on the authority of the city charter and was carried out by the highest city official.[69] The city countered that the circumstances of Owen's firing merely resulted from the conduct of the city manager in one particular instance and not from an official policy to deny notice and a hearing to terminate department heads.[70] The Supreme Court agreed with the Eighth Circuit.[71]

Other federal courts have ruled on the question of municipal policy under Section 1983. In *Dominguez* v. *Beame*, two police officers arrested an alleged prostitute for disorderly conduct.[72] The basis for the arrest was the prostitute's "hassling" of one man who complained to the police and her conversing with three other men on the street. The district court found that the officers lacked probable cause to make an arrest. The Second Circuit, confronting the question of the city's liability for the unconstitutional action, found none.

> "The evidence in this case is clear that although there was a policy to arrest women suspected of being prostitutes on the charge of disorderly conduct, the policy was to arrest only those women actually observed engaging in activity which the police in good faith believed constituted an offense." . . . This . . . disposes of appellant's claim that the Department should be held liable for the fact that she was arrested without probable cause. There was no departmental policy, and there was no showing of a departmental custom, to arrest suspected prostitutes under the "disorderly conduct" statute in the absence of probable cause. The fact that the police officers actually did arrest the appellant without probable cause is a matter to be considered in connection with the officers' individual liability for that arrest, not in connection with the Department's liability.[73]

Compare *Dominguez* with *Sala* v. *County of Suffolk*, where the Second Circuit found that a county police department's procedure for conducting a strip search on all arrestees amounted to municipal policy.[74] And in another recent case, *Turpin* v. *Mailet*, the Second Circuit ruled that a city's tacit approval of police harassment can amount to official policy, even in the absence of a persistent pattern or practice of misconduct.[75] Judge Mansfield explained that a policy can stem from senior officials' implied approval or encouragement of misconduct toward one particular plaintiff. But the court held the plaintiff to a strict standard of proof. As such, Turpin failed to marshal sufficient evidence that his second unlawful arrest stemmed from official policy. His sole evidence consisted of a few comments made by officers after his second arrest, and the fact that the first arresting officer was not disciplined by the board of police commissioners. Despite the publicity surrounding his first arrest and prior lawsuit, Turpin was unable to demonstrate either a connection between the board's failure to discipline the first arresting officer and Turpin's second unlawful arrest, or a pattern of harassment by officers, or an animus toward him in particular that was or should have been known to the board. Thus, the court concluded that the second arrest was not in fact made pursuant to an official municipal policy.

Turpin can be read to hold that a pattern of police misconduct, although not required as a matter of law to establish official policy, may be required as a matter of proof. Thus, a decision expressly authorized by high city or departmental officials, or a clear pattern of employee conduct implicitly approved by the police administration, seems to constitute official policy. Conversely, a mistaken arrest by random officers does not.[76]

Does the burden rest with the plaintiff to allege official policy, custom, or usage?

Yes. Failure to make the necessary allegations may be a defense to the lawsuit.[77]

Can a municipality invoke the good-faith defense in Section 1983 actions?

No. In *Owen* v. *City of Independence*, the Supreme Court ruled that localities may not defend Section 1983 lawsuits on the ground that their employees acted reasonably and in good faith.[78] *Owen* is sure to increase municipal liability for constitutional torts committed in connection with official municipal policy, regardless of whether the challenged act resulted from good intentions and reasonably appeared to be constitutional at the time. Concomitantly, *Owen* is certain to increase employee accountability and enhance the protection of constitutional values by making city employees more careful to avoid violating citizens' rights. Justice Brennan wrote for the majority:

> The central aim of [§1983] was to provide protection to those persons wronged by the "[m]isuse of power, possessed by virtue of state law." . . . How "uniquely amiss" it would be, therefore, if the government itself . . . were permitted to disavow liability for the injury it has begotten. . . . A damages remedy against the offending party is a vital component of any scheme for vindicating cherished constitutional guarantees. . . . Yet owing to the qualified immunity enjoyed by most government officials [when sued as individuals under §1983], . . . many victims of municipal malfeasance would be left remediless if the city were also allowed to assert a good-faith defense. . . . [T]he injustice of such a result should not be tolerated. . . . *The knowledge that a municipality will be liable for all of its injurious conduct, whether committed in good faith or not, should create an incentive for officials who may harbor doubts about the lawfulness of their intended actions to err on the side of protecting citizens' constitutional rights.* Furthermore, the threat that damages might be levied against the city may encourage those in a policymaking position to *institute internal rules and programs designed to minimize the likelihood of infringements on constitutional rights.*[79]

Justice Powell warned in dissent that "local governments and their officials will face the unnerving prospect of crushing damage judgments whenever a policy valid under current law is later found to be unconstitutional. . . . Basic fairness requires a qualified immunity for municipalities. . . ."[80] But the majority held otherwise.

Can a municipality be sued under Section 1983 for declaratory and injunctive relief as well as for damages?

Yes, but relief of this nature will be granted only under certain conditions.[81]

In *Rizzo* v. *Goode,* the plaintiffs alleged that brutality by members of Philadelphia's police force was pervasive.[82] The federal district court, finding that the plaintiffs' constitutional rights had been invaded, issued an injunction requiring then-Mayor Frank Rizzo and the Philadelphia force to set up formal internal administrative procedures to deal with citizens' complaints of brutality. The Supreme Court reversed and dissolved the injunction. The *Rizzo* Court held that injunctions which implement structural changes in police departments cannot issue unless departmental officials affirmatively encouraged subordinates' misconduct. Under *Rizzo,* federal courts appear to retain the power to enjoin proven constitutional infractions by individual officers, but lack the power to remedy a pattern or practice of violations through a broad court decree unless the police administration condoned the behavior.

Of course, where the police administration is proven culpable, federal courts retain broad powers to order corrective action, and have continued to do so.[83] Moreover, in *Monell* v. *Department of Social Services,* the Supreme Court enhanced the accountability of the police administration by establishing that departments are directly liable under Section 1983 when their official policies are challenged.[84] The factual issue is still the same— whether there was an unconstitutional municipal policy— but *Monell* allows plaintiffs to prevail by showing a general or tacit departmental policy without having to prove express or affirmative approval by particular officials.

Can a state be sued in federal court for injunctive relief or an award of damages under Section 1983?

No.[85] A federal court, however, may provide prospective relief by enjoining state *officials* who are sued in their official capacity under Section 1983.[86] Moreover state officials may be sued for damages in their individual capacity, as long as the damage awards are not effectively paid from the state treasury.[87]

Can federal law enforcement officers be sued for a "constitutional tort"?

Yes. As noted earlier, officers of the federal government cannot be sued under Section 1983. They can be sued for damages in a suit which alleges a direct constitutional violation. In *Bivens* v. *Six Unknown Named Agents for the Federal Bureau of Narcotics,* the Supreme Court ruled that federal narcotics agents may be held liable for violating the Fourth Amendment's prohibition against unreasonable searches and seizures.[88] Extending *Bivens,* in *Davis* v. *Passman* the Supreme Court allowed an action against a U.S. Representative for violation of the Fifth Amendment's due-process clause.[89] Similarly, in *Carlson* v. *Green,* the Supreme Court permitted a direct claim under the Eighth Amendment where the plaintiff alleged that a denial of proper medical attention in federal prison constituted cruel and unusual punishment.[90] Interestingly, the *Carlson* Court allowed a "Bivens action" even though the plaintiff's allegations could also support a suit against the United States under the Federal Tort Claims Act.[91] It has not yet been finally determined, however, whether a Bivens action will lie for each and every constitutional violation by a federal officer. Courts have allowed suits against federal officials alleging violations of the First Amendment [92] and the privilege against self-incrimination,[93] but not all courts agree.[94]

Federal officials who are guilty of misconduct may also be held liable under federal statutes. Federal officials who authorize warrantless wiretaps, for example, may be sued for damages under the federal wiretapping statute.[95]

Can a federal official sued in a Bivens action claim a good-faith defense?

Yes. The Supreme Court has expressly held that individual Bivens defendants are entitled to a good-faith defense.[96] Federal law enforcement officers sued under the federal wiretapping statute also may claim the good-faith defense.[97]

May the United States government be sued for the misconduct of federal law-enforcement officers?

Yes. In 1974, Congress amended the Federal Tort Claims Act to permit suits against the government for the intentional torts usually associated with police misconduct.[98] These include false imprisonment, assault and battery. Discretionary acts are excluded from the reach of the statute, but most police misconduct, unless administrative, does not fall within the exempt discretionary category.[99]

What must the plaintiff prove to prevail under the Federal Tort Claims Act?

A plaintiff must demonstrate that the challenged act constitutes a tort under the law of the state where the act occurred (or perhaps under the law of the state in which the court is situated). Once tortious conduct is demonstrated, the federal government becomes liable as would a private individual. Punitive damages cannot be assessed under the Federal Tort Claims Act, however. Nor may either party demand a jury trial, although an advisory jury may be impaneled.

The Federal Tort Claims Act redresses state torts, and does not specifically address constitutional violations. Constitutional deprivations by a police officer, however, often double as state torts—traditionally false imprisonment, assault, and battery. Less traditional misconduct may also be remedied under the federal statute. In *Cruikshank* v. *United States,* for example, the federal district court in Hawaii held that the Federal Tort Claims Act provided a remedy when the CIA opened plaintiff's first-class mail to and from the Soviet Union.[100]

Is the federal government entitled to rely on the good-faith defense in a suit under the Federal Tort Claims Act?

The answer is uncertain. One district court refused to recognize a good-faith defense on the part of the government, but its decision was reversed by the federal court of appeals.[101] Furthermore, although the Supreme Court reasoned in *Owen* v. *City of Independence* that "many victims of [federal employee] malfeasance would be left remediless if the [government, like its individual employees] were also allowed to assert a good-faith defense," [102] it is unclear whether the Court's interpretation of Section 1983, a civil-rights statute, would be applied to the federal tort statute.

Are compensatory damages available to the Section 1983 plaintiff?

Yes. Plaintiffs may recover for actual economic loss, such as medical expenses and lost wages, as well as for emotional and mental distress.[103]

Are compensatory damages allowed in Section 1983 suits in the absence of economic or emotional injury to the plaintiff?

Probably not, although the answer is unclear. In *Carey* v. *Piphus*,[104] the Supreme Court allowed only nominal damages where the plaintiff demonstrated a due-process violation but did not suffer actual harm. Earlier cases had allowed damage awards even though actual loss was lacking, reasoning that a constitutional right is "so valuable that damages are presumed from the wrongful deprivation of it." [105]

Can Section 1983 plaintiffs recover punitive damages?

Yes. Punitive damages are assessed not to compensate the plaintiff for actual loss but to punish the defendant and deter future wrongdoing.[106] They may be awarded in Section 1983 actions where "the defendant acted . . . with actual knowledge that he was violating [a federal right] or . . . with reckless disregard of whether he was violating a right." [107] Although the law is clear that punitive damages can be awarded against individual Section 1983 defendants, in *City of Newport* v. *Facts Concerts, Inc.* the Supreme Court agreed to decide whether municipalities, also, can be assessed punitive damage awards.[108]

Are losing Section 1983 defendants responsible for paying the plaintiff's attorneys' fees?

Yes. The Civil Rights Attorneys' Fee Act of 1976[109] authorizes an award of attorneys' fees to the "prevailing party" in a Section 1983 action. The Supreme Court has confirmed that fee awards should be routinely granted to prevailing plaintiffs,[110] including those who prevail through a settlement.

Can a city, or state officials sued in their official capacity, be ordered to pay the Section 1983 plaintiff's attorneys' fees?

Yes.[111] In *Hutto* v. *Finney*, the Supreme Court permitted an award of attorneys' fees against state corrections officers who were sued in their official capacities. A federal court may order that these fees be paid out of the state treasury.

Can winning Section 1983 defendants recover their own attorneys' fees and costs of suit?

Not unless the plaintiff's Section 1983 claim was utterly frivolous. The Attorneys' Fee Act authorizes the award of fees to a "prevailing party" in a Section 1983 action. In interpreting that Act and an analogous provision in Title VII of the 1964 Civil Rights Act, the Supreme Court has ruled that to encourage the enforcement of civil-rights statutes by private individuals, courts should not award attorneys' fees to "prevailing" defendants unless the plaintiff's claim was frivolous, unreasonable and without foundation.[112]

Can police officers or departments carry insurance against liability in Section 1983 actions?

Generally, yes. In *Hartford Accident and Indemnity Co.* v. *Village of Hempstead,* however, the New York Court of Appeals held that insurance coverage of punitive damages assessed against police officers in civil-rights actions (including Section 1983 suits) violated public policy and was prohibited.[113] The court reasoned that insurance coverage defeated the purposes of punitive damages: to punish defendants and deter others. The *Hartford* decision applies (unless overruled by legislation) to police officers in the State of New York; other states may not follow New York's lead. It should be stressed that *Hartford* does not prohibit insurance coverage of other types of liability.

Can a department or locality be required to indemnify a police officer or pay the costs of defending the lawsuit?

That depends upon the state or local law in an officer's jurisdiction. A New York statute, for example, provides for the indemnification from financial loss of a police officer who is sued in federal court "for damages arising out of a negligent act or failure to act or tort."[114] The statute also provides for the defense of the lawsuit by the city's lawyers if the officer properly notifies the city of the suit.[115] Indemnification cannot be made until a departmental disciplinary proceeding which arises out of the challenged conduct (if any) is resolved in favor of the officer.[116]

The New York state statute only applies to police officers employed in cities having a population over one million.[117] Where state statutes do not provide indemnity, city ordinances, departmental regulations, employment contracts, or union rules may do so. If not, officers cannot force the government or unions to pay liability awards and litigation expenses. Then, officers should resort to personal insurance coverage.

May plaintiffs file a Section 1983 action in either federal or state court?

Yes. Both forums are available to enforce Section 1983 claims.[118]

Can state tort claims be brought in both federal and state courts?

That depends. A state tort claim cannot be pursued in federal court unless the plaintiff and defendant reside in different states,[119] or the federal court in its discretion decides to entertain the plaintiff's state tort claim because it arises from the same factual situation as a Section 1983 claim or a Bivens action [120]—a frequent overlap.

May aliens as well as citizens be plaintiffs in Section 1983 actions?

Yes. Section 1983 protects any "person" who is deprived of a constitutional right under color of state law.[121]

If a lawsuit is not instituted within a prescribed time period, does the plaintiff's delay constitute a defense to the suit?

Yes. Lawsuits of almost every nature must be brought within a prescribed time period, called a "statute of limitations," or else the action will be dismissed. Generally, the statute of limitations in a Section 1983 action is borrowed from an analogous state limitations statute, such as that applicable to actions for assault, battery, false imprisonment, or negligence.[122] It is usually one, two, or three years from the date of the challenged act.[123]

Statutes also often require that a notice of claim be filed with a state or locality within a specified (usually short) period after the challenged act.[124] Where notice is not timely filed, the government may have a defense to a state tort claim, but not to a Section 1983 count.

NOTES

1. Kings: see Scheuer v. Rhodes, 416 U.S. 232, 239 (1974). Judges: Stump v. Sparkman, 435 U.S. 348 (1978) (judge who ordered sterilization of minor without notice, hearing, or appointment of guardian held immune); Pierson v. Ray, 386 U.S. 547 (1967) (absolute immunity from damage actions for official judicial acts). Prosecutors: Imbler v. Pachtman, 424 U.S. 409 (1976) (state prosecutor absolutely immune from liability for acts within scope of employment).

2. Scheuer v. Rhodes, 416 U.S. 232 (1974). Pierson v. Ray, 386 U.S. 547 (1967). Bivens v. Six Unknown Named Agents, 456 F.2d 1339 (2d Cir. 1972) (on remand).

3. Scheuer v. Rhodes, 416 U.S. at 247–48. Accord, Wood v. Strickland, 420 U.S. 308 (1975).

4. E.g., Ore. Const. art. IV, §24. Sala v. County of Suffolk, 604 F.2d 207, 211 n. 5 (2d Cir. 1979), vacated, 48 U.S.L.W. 3673 (U.S. Apr. 21, 1980) (No. 79–620). See generally W. PROSSER, THE LAW OF TORTS §131, at 977–79 (4th ed. 1971).

5. Scheuer v. Rhodes, 416 U.S. at 239. Cf. Owen v. City of Independence, 48 U.S.L.W. 4389, 4395–96 & n. 28 (U.S. Apr. 15, 1980).

6. Id. PROSSER, supra note 4, §131, at 977–80, 984–87. E.g., 1979 MASS. ACTS ch. 512; N.Y. GEN. MUN. LAW art. 4, §50–j(1) (1977); Stone v. Arizona Highway Comm'n, 93 Ariz. 384, 381 P.2d 107 (1963); Muskopf v. Corning Hosp. Dist., 55 Cal. 2d 211, 359 P.2d 457 (1961).

7. N.Y. GEN MUN. LAW art. 4, §50–j(1) (1977). See Domino v. Mercurio, 17 App. Div. 2d 342, 234 N.Y.S. 2d 1011 (4th Dep't 1962); Bernardine v. City of New York, 294 N.Y. 361 (1945).

8. 28 U.S.C. §§2671–80 (1976).

9. Scheuer v. Rhodes, 416 U.S. at 239.

10. Id. at 240. Accord, Sala v. County of Suffolk, 604 F.2d at 208–11.

11. 42 U.S.C. §1983 (1976).
12. Gomez v. Toledo, 48 U.S.L.W. 4600, 4601 (U.S. May 27, 1980). Popow v. City of Margate, 476 F. Supp. 1237 (D.N.J. 1979). Loopman v. Hurley, 475 F. Supp. 98 (D.N.H. 1979) (more than ordinary negligence needed to state a constitutional claim against police officer for leaving unattended a prisoner who was asphyxiated in his own vomit and died). See Maine v. Thiboutot, 48 U.S.L.W. 4859 (U.S. June 25, 1980) (§1983 encompasses claims based on purely federal statutory violations). See also Owens v. Haas, 601 F.2d 1242, 1245–47 (2d Cir. 1979) (regarding county or municipality, plaintiff must show "gross negligence" or "deliberate indifference" in defendant's training and supervision of police officers in order to state claim under §1983).
13. Popow v. City of Margate, 476 F. Supp. 1237 (D.N.J. 1979).
14. See Bivens v. Six Unknown Named Agents, 403 U.S. 388 (1971).
15. N. DORSEN, P. BENDER, B. NEUBORNE & J. GORA, EMERSON, HABER AND DORSEN'S POLITICAL AND CIVIL RIGHTS IN THE UNITED STATES 354 (Supp. 1980) (hereinafter DORSEN & NEUBORNE SUPP.). See Flagg Bros., Inc. v. Brooks, 436 U.S. 149 (1978).
16. 522 F.2d 438 (6th Cir. 1975), 429 U.S. 118 (1976) (dismissing certiorari as improvidently granted).
17. United States v. Classic, 313 U.S. 299, 326 (1941).
18. See Kotmair v. Gray, 505 F.2d 744 (4th Cir. 1974); Henderson v. Thrower, 497 F.2d 125 (5th Cir. 1974).
19. District of Columbia v. Carter, 409 U.S. 418 (1973).
20. Act of Dec. 31, 1979, Pub. L. No. 96–170, 93 Stat. 1284 (codified at 42 U.S.C.A. §1983 (West. Supp. 1980)).
21. W. Prosser, supra note 4, §31, at 145–49.
22. Id. §10, at 37–41.
23. Id. §9, at 34–37.
24. Id. §11, at 42–49.
25. Id. §30, at 143–45.
26. 296 N.Y. 99, 71 N.E.2d 419 (1947).
27. Popow v. City of Margate, 476 F. Supp. 1237 (D.N.J. 1979). Accord, Owens v. Haas, 601 F.2d 1242 (2d Cir. 1979).
28. E.g., 42 U.S.C. §§1981, 1985(3) (1976).
29. 1979 Mass. Acts ch. 801.

30. *See* Maine v. Thiboutot, 48 U.S.L.W. 4859 (U.S. June 25, 1980); Chapman v. Houston Welfare Rights Org., 441 U.S. 600 (1979); Paul v. Davis, 424 U.S. 693 (1976); Tucker v. Duncan, 499 F.2d 963 (4th Cir. 1974); Butler v. Bensinger, 377 F. Supp. 870 (N.D. Ill. 1974).

31. In Parratt v. Taylor, 49 U.S.L.W. 3289 (U.S. Oct. 20, 1980) (No. 79–1734) (granting petition for certiorari), the Supreme Court agreed to review the question whether simple negligence may form the basis of a §1983 count. The Court also agreed to review the issue whether certain property owned by §1983 plaintiffs might be of such minimal value that its deprivation is not remediable under that statute.

32. 424 U.S. 693 (1976).

33. 429 U.S. 97 (1976).

34. 443 U.S. 137 (1979).

35. Popow v. City of Margate, 476 F. Supp. 1237 (D.N.J. 1979).

36. 49 U.S.L.W. 3289 (U.S. Oct. 20, 1980) (No. 79–1734).

37. *See* note 31 *supra;* Popow v. City of Margate, 476 F. Supp. 1237 (D.N.J. 1979) (no); Loopman v. Hurley, 475 F. Supp. 98 (D.N.H. 1979) (no); *cf.* Owens v. Haas, 601 F.2d 1242, 1245–47 (2d Cir. 1979) (no as to counties and localities).

38. Estelle v. Gamble, 429 U.S. 97 (1976).

39. *See* Popow v. City of Margate, 476 F. Supp. 1237 (D.N.J. 1979); Loopman v. Hurley, 475 F. Supp. 98 (D.N.H. 1979); *cf.* Owens v. Haas, 601 F.2d 1242, 1245–47 (2d Cir. 1979).

40. 386 U.S. 547 (1967). *Accord,* Procunier v. Navarette, 434 U.S. 555 (1978) (prison officials); Scheuer v. Rhodes, 416 U.S. 232 (1974) (State governor and executives). *See* Tucker v. Maher, 497 F.2d. 1309 (2d Cir. 1974). *Cf.* Bivens v. Six Unknown Named Agents, 456 F.2d 1339 (2d Cir. 1972) (on remand).

41. 420 U.S. 308, 321–22 (1975).

42. Bivens v. Six Unknown Named Agents, 456 F.2d at 1348. *Accord,* Dominguez v. Beame, 603 F.2d 337 (2d Cir. 1979), *cert. denied,* 48 U.S.L.W. 3696 (U.S. Apr. 29, 1980).

43. *See* Gomez v. Toledo, 48 U.S.L.W. 4600, 4601 (U.S. May 27, 1980).

44. Procunier v. Navarette, 434 U.S. 555, 562 (1978).

45. Scheuer v. Rhodes, 416 U.S. at 245. *See* Bivens v. Six Unknown Named Agents, 456 F.2d 1339 (2d Cir. 1972) (on remand) (violation of Fourth Amendment's proscription of unreasonable searches and seizures).

46. *Compare* Aldridge v. Mullins, 377 F. Supp. 850 (M.D. Tenn. 1972), *aff'd*, 474 F.2d 1189 (6th Cir. 1973) (good-faith defense unavailable in §1983 action when based upon assault and battery rather than false arrest, false imprisonment, or malicious prosecution, as defense not available under common law), *with* Mattis v. Schnarr, 502 F.2d 588 (8th Cir. 1974), *vacated on other grounds sub nom.* Ashcroft v. Mattis, 431 U.S. 171 (1977) (per curiam) (defense available), *and* Jones v. Marshall, 383 F. Supp. 358 (D. Conn. 1974) (defense available).

47. *See* Dalehite v. United States, 346 U.S. 15 (1953); Chandler v. District of Columbia, 48 U.S.L.W. 2131 (D.C. Ct. App. Aug. 2, 1979).

48. 48 U.S.L.W. 4076, 4077 (U.S. Jan. 15, 1980), (citations and footnotes omitted).

49. Owen v. City of Independence, 48 U.S.L.W. 4389, 4396 & n. 30 (U.S. Apr. 15, 1980). Martinez v. California, 48 U.S.L.W. 4076, 4077–78 & n. 8 (U.S. Jan. 15, 1980). Hampton v. City of Chicago, 484 F.2d 602, 607 (7th Cir. 1973), *cert. denied*, 415 U.S. 917 (1974). *See* Spence v. Staras, 507 F.2d 554 (7th Cir. 1974); Joyce v. Gilligan, 383 F. Supp. 1028 (N.D. Ohio 1974), *aff'd mem.*, 510 F.2d 973 (6th Cir. 1975).

50. Martinez v. California, 48 U.S.L.W. 4076, 4077–78 & n. 8 (U.S. Jan. 15, 1980).

51. 48 U.S.L.W. 4600 (U.S. May 27, 1980), *impliedly overruling* Sala v. County of Suffolk, 604 F.2d 207, 209 (2d Cir. 1979), *vacated on other grounds*, 48 U.S.L.W. 3673 (U.S. Apr. 21, 1980) (No. 79–620), *and* Cruz v. Beto, 603 F.2d 1178 (5th Cir. 1979). *See* Bivens v. Six Unknown Named Agents, 456 F.2d at 1348 (on remand) ("the officer must allege and prove [good faith and reasonableness]").

52. 48 U.S.L.W. at 4601.

53. *See id.;* Bivens v. Six Unknown Named Agents, 456 F.2d at 1348. *But cf.* Gomez v. Toledo, 48 U.S.L.W. at 4602 (Rehnquist, J., concurring).

54. *Id.* (Rehnquist, J., concurring) (leaving open question of burden of proof).

55. Cruz v. Beto, 603 F.2d 1178 (5th Cir. 1979).
56. See, e.g., Rowley v. McMillan, 502 F.2d 1326 (4th Cir. 1974).
57. See Ex parte Young, 209 U.S. 123, 159–60 (1908). Cf. Aland v. Graham, 287 Ala. 226, 250 So.2d 677 (1971); O'Neil v. Thomson, 114 N.H. 155, 316 A.2d 168 (1974); Gast v. Oregon, 36 Ore. App. 441, 585 P.2d 12 (1978).
58. See Ex parte Young, 209 U.S. 123, 159–60 (1908).
59. Bertot v. School Dist. No. 1, 48 U.S.L.W. 2407 (10th Cir. Dec. 18, 1979).
60. See id. Cf. Paxman v. Campbell, 48 U.S.L.W. 2451 (4th Cir. Jan. 2, 1980) (qualified immunity applies to equitable relief).
61. Monroe v. Pape, 367 U.S. 167 (1961), overruled in part, Monell v. Department of Social Services, 436 U.S. 658 (1978).
62. 436 U.S. 658 (1978).
63. Id. at 690–91 (citations and footnotes omitted). Accord, Dominguez v. Beame, 603 F.2d 337 (2d Cir. 1979); cert. denied, 48 U.S.L.W. 3696 (U.S. Apr. 29, 1980); Baskin v. Parker, 602 F.2d 1205 (5th Cir. 1979) (sheriff not vicariously liable for deputy sheriff's unlawful procurement and execution of a search warrant); Solimini v. City of Quincy, Mass. Lawyers Weekly No. B77 (D. Mass. 1980) (municipality not liable where plaintiff police officer failed to allege that city maintained unconstitutional policy, custom, or usage).
64. See text accompanying notes 4–10, 43–47 supra.
65. 48 U.S.L.W. 2131 (D.C. Ct. App. Aug. 2, 1979).
66. Owen v. City of Independence, 48 U.S.L.W. 4389, 4397 (U.S. Apr. 15, 1980).
67. Turpin v. Mailet, 48 U.S.L.W. 2714 (2d Cir. Apr. 8, 1980) (Mansfield, J.). Accord, Familias Unidas v. Briscoe, 619 F.2d 391 (5th Cir., 1980); Echols v. Strickland, 49 U.S.L.W. 2275 (S.D. Tex. Sept. 26, 1980). See Lyons v. City of Los Angeles, 615 F.2d 1243 (9th Cir. 1980), cert. denied, 49 U.S.L.W. 3288 (U.S. Oct. 20, 1980) (No. 79–1995) (victim of police stranglehold could sue municipality to prevent future use of technique in all arrest situations except where deadly force is threatened).
68. 48 U.S.L.W. 4389 (U.S. Apr. 15, 1980).
69. 589 F.2d 335 (8th Cir. 1978).

70. 48 U.S.L.W. 3445–46 (editorial summary of oral argument).

71. *See* 48 U.S.L.W. at 4392 & n. 13.

72. 603 F.2d 337 (2d Cir. 1979), *cert. denied,* 48 U.S.L.W. 3696 (U.S. Apr. 29, 1980).

73. *Id.* at 341–42.

74. 604 F.2d 207, 211 (2d Cir. 1979), *vacated,* 48 U.S.L.W. 3673 (U.S. Apr. 21, 1980). (No. 79–620). *See also* Logan v. Schealy, 49 U.S.L.W. 2260 (E.D. Va. Sept. 30, 1980) (strip search policy held constitutional).

75. Turpin v. Mailet, 48 U.S.L.W. 2714 (2d Cir. Apr. 8, 1980).

76. Dominguez v. Beame, 603 F.2d 337 (2d Cir. 1979), *cert. denied,* 48 U.S.L.W. 3696 (U.S. Apr. 29, 1980). *See* Baskin v. Parker, 602 F.2d 1205 (5th Cir. 1979). *Cf.* Turpin v. Mailet, 48 U.S.L.W. 2714 (2d Cir. Apr. 8, 1980).

77. Dominguez v. Beame, 603 F.2d at 341. *See* Solimini v. City of Quincy, Mass. Lawyers Weekly No. B77 (D. Mass. 1980) (municipality not liable where plaintiff police officer failed to allege that city maintained policy, custom, or usage that interfered with First Amendment rights).

78. 48 U.S.L.W. 4389 (U.S. Apr. 16, 1980) (Brennan, White, Marshall, Blackmun & Stevens, JJ.). *Accord,* Sala v. City of Suffolk, 48 U.S.L.W. 3673 (U.S. Apr. 21, 1980) (No. 79–620), *vacating* 604 F.2d 207 (2d Cir. 1979); Bertot v. School Dist. No. 1, 48 U.S.L.W. 2407 (10th Cir. Dec. 18, 1979) (en banc) (no immunity in suit for back pay); Hostrop v. Board of Junior College Dist. No. 515, 523 F.2d 569 (7th Cir. 1975); Shuman v. City of Philadelphia, 47 U.S.L.W. 2720 (E.D. Pa. Apr. 18, 1979). *See* Hander v. San Jacinto Junior College, 519 F.2d 273, 277 n. 1 (5th Cir. 1975).

79. 48 U.S.L.W. at 4397 (emphasis added; citations & footnotes omitted).

80. *Id. at* 4399 (Powell, Stewart, Rehnquist, JJ. & Burger, C.J.).

81. Monell v. Department of Social Services, 436 U.S. 658, 690–91 (1978).

82. 423 U.S. 362 (1976). *See* Lewis v. Hyland, 544 F.2d 93 (3d Cir. 1977).

83. *See* Lyons v. City of Los Angeles, 615 F.2d 1243 (9th Cir. 1980), *cert. denied,* 49 U.S.L.W. 3288 (U.S. Oct.

20, 1980) (No. 70–1995) (enjoining departmental use of stranglehold in non-life-threatening situations); Illinois Migrant Council v. Pilliod, 540 F.2d 1062 (7th Cir. 1976), *modified* 548 F.2d 715 (7th Cir. 1977); Pennsylvania v. Porter, 480 F. Supp. 686 (W.D. Pa. 1979); Shifrin v. Wilson, 412 F. Supp. 1282 (D.D.C. 1976); Cicero v. Ogliati, 410 F. Supp. 1080 (S.D.N.Y. 1976); Tucker v. City of Montgomery Bd. of Comm'rs, 410 F. Supp. 494 (M.D. Ala. 1976).

84. 436 U.S. 658 (1978).

85. Quern v. Jordan, 440 U.S. 332 (1979). Edelman v. Jordan, 415 U.S. 651 (1974).

86. *Id.* at 664. *Ex parte* Young, 209 U.S. 123 (1908). *See* Hutto v. Finney, 437 U.S. 678, 690 (1978).

87. *See* Edelman v. Jordan, 415 U.S. at 663, 668.

88. 403 U.S. 388 (1971).

89. 442 U.S. 228 (1979).

90. 48 U.S.L.W. 4425 (U.S. Apr. 22, 1980). *See* Waltenberg v. New York City Department of Corrections, 376 F. Supp. 41 (S.D.N.Y. 1974); Walker v. McCune, 363 F. Supp. 254 (E.D. Va. 1973).

91. 48 U.S.L.W. 4425 (U.S. Apr. 22, 1980). A bill was introduced in the 96th Congress to overrule *Carlson*'s holding that the Federal Tort Claims Act does not provide an exclusive remedy for misconduct by federal employees. H.R. 2659, H.R. 7475, & S. 1858, 96th Cong., 2d Sess. (1980). The bill passed the Senate but died in the House.

92. Peacock v. Board of Regents, 380 F. Supp. 1081 (D. Ariz. 1974).

93. Shaffer v. Wilson, 383 F. Supp. 554 (D. Colo. 1974).

94. *Cf.* Smothers v. CBS, 351 F. Supp. 622 (C.D. Cal. 1972) (no cause of action under First Amendment against private parties).

95. 18 U.S.C. §2510 *et seq. See* Zweibon v. Mitchell, 48 U.S.L.W. 2052 (D.C. Cir. July 12, 1979), *petition for cert. filed*, 48 U.S.L.W. 3404 (U.S. Dec. 7, 1979) (No. 79–881, 883); Halperin v. Kissinger, 48 U.S.L.W. 2050 (D.C. Cir. July 12, 1979), *petition for cert. granted*, 48 U.S.L.W. 3750 (U.S. May 19, 1980) (No. 79–880); Nixon v. Smith, —— F.2d —— (D.C. Cir, July 12, 1979), *petition for cert. filed*, 48 U.S.L.W. 3404 (U.S. Dec. 7, 1979) (No. 79–882).

96. Butz v. Economou, 438 U.S. 478 (1978). G. M. Leasing Co. v. United States, 429 U.S. 338 (1977).

97. Halperin v. Kissinger, 48 U.S.L.W. 2050 (D.C. Cir. July 12, 1979), *petition for cert. granted,* 48 U.S.L.W. 3750 (U.S. May 19, 1980) (No. 79–880); Forsyth v. Kleindienst, 599 F.2d 1203 (3d Cir. 1979), *petition for cert. filed,* 48 U.S.L.W. 3481 (Jan. 21, 1980) (No. 79–1120).

98. 28 U.S.C. §2680(h) (1976).

99. *Id.* §2680(a). *Accord.* Dalehite v. United States, 346 U.S. 15 (1953). *See,* DORSEN & NEUBORNE SUPP, *supra* note 15, at 333–36.

100. 431 F. Supp. 1355 (D. Hawaii 1977).

101. Norton v. Turner, 427 F. Supp. 138 (E.D. Va. 1976), *rev'd,* 581 F.2d 390 (4th Cir.), *cert. denied,* 439 U.S. 1003 (1978).

102. 48 U.S.L.W. at 4397.

103. Basista v. Weir, 340 F.2d 74 (3d Cir. 1965). *See* Halperin v. Kissinger, 48 U.S.L.W. 2050 (D.C. Cir. July 12, 1979), *petition for cert. granted,* 48 U.S.L.W. 3750 (U.S. May 19, 1980) (No. 79–880) (where federal constitutional tort alleged, plaintiffs can recover for loss due to emotional distress and mental anguish); cases cited at 1 N. DORSEN, P. BENDER, & B. NEUBORNE, EMERSON, HABER, and DORSEN'S POLITICAL AND CIVIL RIGHTS IN THE UNITED STATES 1305–06, §8 (4th ed. 1976) (hereinafter DORSEN & NEUBORNE).

104. 435 U.S. 247 (1978).

105. Wayne v. Venable, 260 F. 64, 66 (8th Cir. 1919) (Sanborn, J.).

106. Hartford Accident & Indemnity Co. v. Village of Hempstead, 48 U.S.L.W. 2325 (N.Y. Ct. App. Oct 13, 1979).

107. Adickes v. S. H. Kress & Co., 398 U.S. 144, 232–33 (1970) (Opinion of Brennan, J.). *See* McDaniel v. Carroll, 457 F.2d 968 (6th Cir. 1972); Basista v. Weir, 340 F.2d 74 (3d Cir. 1965); cases cited at DORSEN & NEUBORNE, *supra* note 103, at 1306–07, §9.

108. 49 U.S.L.W. 3440 (U.S. Dec. 15, 1980) (No. 80–396) (granting petition for certiorari).

109. 42 U.S.C. §1988 (1976).

110. *See* Maher v. Gagne, 48 U.S.L.W. 4891 (U.S. June 25, 1980); Christiansburg Garment Co. v. EEOC, 434 U.S.

412, 416–17 (1977); Newman v. Piggie Park Enterprises, 390 U.S. 400 (1968) (per curiam).

111. 42 U.S.C. §1988 (1976). Hutto v. Finney, 437 U.S. 678, 691–92 (1978). Gates v. Collier, 48 U.S.L.W. 2810 (5th Cir. May 4, 1980) (court has authority to order state treasury to pay attorneys' fees). See Entertainment Concepts, Inc. III v. Maciejewski, 49 U.S.L.W. 2242 (7th Cir. Sept. 23, 1980); Mirrosn v. Ayoob, 49 U.S.L.W. 2098 (3d Cir. July 29, 1980). Cf. Fitzgerald v. Bitzer, 427 U.S. 445 (1976).

112. See Hughes v. Rowe, 49 U.S.L.W. 3346 (U.S. Nov. 10, 1980) (per curiam); Christiansburg Garment Co. v. EEOC, 434 U. S. 412 (1977). See also Baker v. Detroit, 49 U.S.L.W. 2387 (E.D. Mich. Nov. 17, 1980) (defendants and intervenors in "reverse" discrimination suit can be awarded attorney's fees though plaintiff's suit not frivolous).

113. U.S.L.W. 2325 (N.Y. Ct. App. Oct. 13, 1979).

114. N.Y. GEN. MUN. LAW art. 4, §50–k(2) (1977).

115. Id. §50–k(3).

116. Id. §50–k(5).

117. Id. §50–k(1)(a).

118. See Davis v. Towe, 379 F. Supp. 536 (E.D. Va. 1974), aff'd mem., 526 F.2d 558 (4th Cir. 1975). But cf. Martinez v. California, 48 U.S.L.W. 4076, 4077 (U.S. Jan. 15, 1980).

119. 28 U.S.C. §1332 (1976).

120. See United Mine Workers v. Gibbs, 383 U.S. 715 (1966) (pendent jurisdiction).

121. Jagnandan v. Giles, 379 F. Supp. 1178 (N.D. Miss. 1974), aff'd, 538 F.2d 1166 (5th Cir. 1976), cert. denied, 432 U.S. 910 (1977).

122. Regan v. Sullivan, 557 F.2d 300 (2d Cir. 1977); Polite v. Diehl, 507 F.2d 119 (3d Cir. 1974); Holly v. Alliance Rubber Co., 380 F. Supp. 1128 (N.D. Ohio 1974); Marshall v. Chrysler Corp., 379 F. Supp. 94 (E.D. Mich. 1974).

123. E.g., Regan v. Sullivan, 557 F.2d 300 (2d Cir. 1977) (three-year statute of limitations for §1983 actions brought in New York).

124. N.Y. GEN. MUN. LAW art. 4, §50–(j)(3) (1977).

IX

Miscellaneous Rights and Duties

A. THE DUTY TO PREVENT CRIME

Do police officers owe a duty to individuals to prevent crime?

Usually not.

By statute, police officers owe a general duty to the public as a whole to prevent crime.[1] This duty, however, does not in most instances run to individual members of society. Accordingly, a municipality and its police officers are not ordinarily liable in tort for failure to provide police protection to an individual.[2] Similarly, failure to provide adequate police protection does not usually amount to a constitutional violation under civil-rights statutes such as Section 1983.[3]

This is true even where someone has specifically requested police protection based upon repeated threats of personal harm. In *Riss* v. *City of New York*, for example, the plaintiff had been repeatedly and seriously threatened by a rejected suitor.[4] At a party celebrating her engagement to another man, she received a telephone threat warning her that it was her "last chance" to prevent danger.[5] Overwrought, she begged the police for help, but was refused. The next day, a thug hired by her rejected suitor threw lye in her face. The plaintiff lost most of her vision, and her face was permanently scarred. After the assault, the police provided around-the-clock protection for the next three and a half years.

In a 6–1 decision, the New York Court of Appeals held that the city was not liable for failing to protect the plaintiff. The court ruled that the case involved "the provision of a governmental service to protect the public generally from external hazards and particularly to control the activities of criminal wrongdoers." [6] As such,

> The amount of protection that may be provided is limited by the resources of the community and by a considered legislative-executive decision as to how those resources may be deployed. For the courts to proclaim a new and general duty of protection in the law of tort, even to those who may be the particular seekers of protection based on specific hazards, could and would inevitably determine how the limited police resources of the community should be allocated and without predictable limits. . . .
>
> Before such extension of responsibilities should be dictated by the indirect imposition of tort liabilities, there should be a legislative determination that that should be the scope of public responsibility.[7]

The dissent advocated a rule holding the city liable where the police had actual notice of danger to the plaintiff and ample opportunity to take remedial steps, but negligently failed to do so.[8] It reasoned that such a properly limited rule would provide compensation for victims under generally accepted tort principles but would prevent a barrage of frivolous litigation instituted by every victim of crime.

Recent cases involving allegations of negligent police or fire protection have included situations (1) where a shop patron was wounded during an armed robbery,[9] (2) where a police department, probation officers, and court clerks refused to arrest or provide protection for wives who were later assaulted by their husbands,[10] and (3) where the District of Columbia's closing of fire stations on a rotating basis affected a station near a fire that resulted in the death of children.[11] In each instance the court refused to find municipal liability. In the second case, however, the police department entered into a consent judgment ending the New York City Police Department's long-standing practice of refusing to arrest violent men who are married to their victims, and requiring the arrest of men who commit felonious assault against their wives.[12]

Are there limited instances where the police or a municipality may be held liable for failure to provide protection to an individual?

Yes. As an exception to the general rule discussed above, the municipality or police may be liable for failure to provide police protection to an individual (1) where the police have developed a "special relationship" with the victim and accordingly owe the victim some measure of protection,[13] and (2) where the police affirmatively undertake to protect an individual but then negligently fail to perform.[14] In either of these two cases, the police may be liable for negligent conduct that results in harm to a victim.

The case of *Schuster* v. *City of New York* [15] exemplifies the first situation. There, an ordinary citizen supplied information to the New York City Police Department leading to the arrest of a dangerous fugitive. The citizen's role in the arrest was widely publicized. He immediately received threats to his life, and notified the police. The police afforded some protection but assured him that the threats were exaggerated.[16] Eighteen days later, the citizen was shot and killed.

The New York Court of Appeals held that the City of New York would be liable in damages for wrongful death if the facts were as charged. The court reasoned that the police owe "a special duty to use reasonable care for the protection of persons who have collaborated with it in the arrest or prosecution of criminals, once it reasonably appears that they are in danger due to their collaboration." "If it were otherwise," the court continued, "it might well become difficult to convince the citizen to aid and co-operate with the law enforcement officers." [17] Moreover, the court reasoned, in such situations the government, in actively seeking law-enforcement help, has affirmatively acted to the degree that failure to provide police protection "would commonly result, not . . . merely in withholding

a benefit, but positively or actively in working an injury." [18]
Hence the Court concluded that the government assumed
the duty to take reasonable measures to protect Schuster
against harm from third persons.

Warren v. *District of Columbia* exemplifies the second
situation: where the police promise but negligently fail
to provide protection.[19] There, two women who heard the
screams of a housemate called the police and were assured
that an officer would be dispatched immediately. They
went to the roof of their home and waited for help. From
their perch they saw one police officer pass the house
without stopping and a second leave their doorway when
no one answered his knocks. The two women re-entered
the house and called the police a second time; again they
were assured that help was on the way. Then, believing
that the police had arrived, they called down to their
housemate. The intruders captured them at knife point
and repeatedly raped and abused them. Police help never
came. The D.C. Court of Appeals ruled that, although
there is a bar against lawsuits alleging a breach of a
general duty to provide police services, a suit can be
brought for negligence in cases of "specific assurances
of protection that give rise to justifiable reliance by the
victim." [20]

Of course, municipalities and police departments may
be held liable for injury caused by their *own* officers.
Such misconduct includes, for example, the negligent
failure to discharge an officer who had a record of repeated drunkenness and who shot and killed a victim while
intoxicated.[21] Police misconduct of this sort is different
from the failure to prevent crime by third parties, and is
accordingly treated separately in Chapter VIII.

**Does Section 1983 give rise to liability for failure to
provide police services?**

Probably not, except in unusual circumstances.

In *Martinez* v. *California,* a fifteen-year-old girl was
murdered by a parolee.[22] The parolee had been convicted
of attempted rape and had been committed to a state mental hospital as a "mentally disordered sex offender not
amenable to treatment." Five years later he was paroled by
state authorities, allegedly in violation of procedures and

against better judgment. Five months after that, he tortured and killed the Martinez girl. Her survivors brought suit under Section 1983, charging that the parole-release decision deprived the victim of her life in violation of the Fourteenth Amendment. The U.S. Supreme Court assumed, as the plaintiffs alleged, that the parole decision was negligent, reckless, willful, and malicious. Nonetheless, the Court refused to find that the parole determination deprived the victim of her life.

> [The victim's] life was taken by the parolee five months after his release. He was in no sense an agent of the parole board. . . . Further, the parole board was not aware that [the victim], as distinguished from the public at large, faced any special danger. We need not and do not decide that a parole officer could never be deemed to "deprive" someone of life by action taken in connection with the release of a prisoner on parole. But we do hold that at least under the particular circumstances of this parole decision, [the victim's] death is too remote a consequence of the parole officer's action to hold them responsible under the federal civil rights law. . . . [Not] every injury in which a state official has played some part is actionable under that statute.[23]

Put another way, a "legislative decision that has an incremental impact on the probability that death will result . . . cannot be characterized as state action depriving a person of life just because it may set in motion a chain of events that ultimately leads to the random death of an innocent bystander." [24]

Note that under the Supreme Court's language in *Martinez*, Section 1983 liability is not necessarily precluded where, as in *Schuster* v. *City of New York*,[25] the police have developed a "special" relationship with the victim resulting in harm which is not "random."

Are police departments liable for crimes committed on premises owned or operated by them?

Yes, if the failure to provide protection was both negligent and a proximate cause of the victim's injuries.[26]

The duty to safeguard premises owned or operated by a police department presents different circumstances from the general provision of protective services to the public or to individuals. Such ownership or operation of facilities might include, for example, a complex of buildings operated by the police and open for use by the public. Here a city, police department, or individual officer would be liable under general tort principles for injuries directly caused by its negligent operations. The basis for liability would be the usual duty of care owed by an owner of land or a business proprietor to those who use the proffered facilities.[27]

In *Kenny* v. *SEPTA*, for example, a patron of the Philadelphia transit system was raped on a train platform that was inadequately lighted and unreasonably far from the visual and hearing range of the sole transit employee on premises.[28] The Third Circuit Court of Appeals upheld an award of damages against the Philadelphia transit authority based on its negligent failure to provide adequate protection on the platform. The Court ruled that a transit authority, like a proprietor of a business establishment or a land owner, may be responsible for injuries to patrons caused by the criminal conduct of third persons if the possibility or likelihood of the criminal activity could have been reasonably anticipated.

By analogy, a police department may be liable for injuries caused by criminal conduct on premises owned or operated by it if such conduct could have been anticipated and prevented by taking reasonable protective measures.

The decision in *Kenny* v. *SEPTA* is framed in terms of the ordinary duty of a landowner to the public. Still, *Kenny* may represent an extension of the police officer's duty to prevent crimes by third parties. Under its reasoning, a city, town, or precinct may be held liable for crimes committed in streets and parks which it "owns" or "operates," if the crime could have been anticipated and should have been prevented by reasonable protective measures.

B. OFFICER VERSUS CITIZEN

While many police officers have found themselves on the defendant's side of a lawsuit, the legal system also allows individual officers to redress wrongs committed against them. Aside from the legal concerns shared by all citizens, there are at least three common-law torts that may be of particular interest to police-officer plaintiffs—battery, malicious prosecution, and abuse of process. Some jurisdictions such as California, however, prevent law-enforcement personnel from recovering damages in tort for personal injuries and death occurring while on duty.[29] Police officers should accordingly consult local law to determine whether they can, for these purposes, sit on the plaintiff's side of the courtroom.

What is battery?

Battery is a common-law tort that consists of intentionally touching another without permission. The person committing the battery therefore must bring about contact with the victim's body (or something attached to it such as clothing). The contact must be intentional; it must not be consented to by the victim; and it must not be justifiable by any of the well-recognized defenses to the tort of battery.[30] These defenses include, among others, self-defense, defense of others, and defense of property.

In what circumstance might a police officer bring a lawsuit for battery?

Suppose a police officer attempts to make a lawful arrest based upon probable cause or pursuant to a validly issued warrant. If the target unlawfully resists the arrest and injures the officer, the officer might sue for battery and seek a monetary award for his or her damages.

What is malicious prosecution?

Malicious prosecution is a common-law tort recognized in most, but not all, jurisdictions in the United States. If a plaintiff starts wrongful (that is, frivolous or unfounded) civil proceedings in one action, the defendant in that case (such as a police officer) can later become the plaintiff in a malicious-prosecution case. The original plaintiff, who proceeded wrongfully, becomes the new defendant. The malicious-prosecution plaintiff must: (1) establish that the former proceeding ended in his favor; (2) prove that the former proceeding was initiated without "probable cause"; (3) prove that the former proceeding was motivated by "malice" of the original plaintiff; and (4) prove actual damages.[31]

In what circumstances might a police officer bring a lawsuit for malicious prosecution?

Suppose Mr. X brings a lawsuit against Officer Y under Section 1983, alleging police brutality. Mr. X knows that Officer Y did not harm him, but dislikes the officer for having arrested him and for testifying against him in a criminal proceeding in which Mr. X was found guilty. Assuming that Mr. X loses his police-brutality lawsuit, Officer Y might then institute a claim for malicious prosecution. The first proceeding terminated in his favor; the proceeding was initiated without probable cause since there were no facts with which Mr. X could support the brutality claim; Mr. X was motivated by "malice," because he probably did not believe his claim would succeed since he knew that Officer Y had not acted improperly; and Officer Y might be able to prove that his reputation in the community was damaged by the brutality suit.

What is abuse of process?

Abuse of process is also a common-law tort. Abuse of process differs from malicious prosecution in that a lawsuit may have been properly begun and been premised on probable cause but "nevertheless has been perverted to accomplish an ulterior purpose for which it was not designed."[32] Thus the abuse-of-process plaintiff need not prove that the proceeding "terminated in his favor, or that the process was obtained without probable cause."[33] Malice need be proved, but only in the sense that process has been invoked for an improper purpose. The typical abuse-of-process situation has entailed the institution of legal proceedings, not to win the lawsuit stated in the complaint, but, for example, to extort payment of a debt.[34] The elements of a claim for abuse of process are "first, an ulterior purpose, and second, a willful act in the use of the process not proper in the regular conduct of the proceeding." [35]

In what circumstances might a police officer bring a lawsuit for abuse of process?

Suppose again that Mr. X swears out a criminal complaint against Officer Y for assault, asserting that during off-duty hours Officer Y struck Mr. X. Mr. X's purpose is not to bring Officer Y to justice, but to deter Officer Y from zealous law enforcement because the police officer has been investigating illegal gambling operations run by Mr. X. It would be appropriate for Officer Y to claim abuse of process, because Mr. X brought suit for an ulterior purpose unrelated to the criminal proceedings.

C. DANGEROUS WORKING CONDITIONS

Police work is often extremely hazardous. Accordingly, police officers and their representatives have vociferously sought changes in working conditions which have been thought to be unnecessarily dangerous. Without minimizing the inherent danger of police work, many police officers have contended that unnecessarily dangerous conditions could be alleviated. Of recent interest—at least to New York City police—have been demands for bulletproof vests and resistance to mandatory duty in one-person patrol cars [36] and in bomb-prone locations.[37]

New York City officials have recently decided to supply all police, including transit, correction, and housing officers, with bulletproof vests.[38] Greater controversy has centered on the decision to have some parts of New York City patrolled by one-officer patrol cars. Many officers have objected to this practice, arguing that it is simply too dangerous. The shooting death of a New York City police officer on January 8, 1980, after 165,000 hours of one-officer car patrols without incident, led to a temporary suspension of their use. The department, whether acknowledging the danger of one-person patrol cars or the anxiety of officers, now allows officers in such cars to carry shot-guns and restricts their use to low-crime areas. The department also requires that officers in one-person patrol cars radio for backup in dangerous situations, although the first instinct of many officers may be to leave the car and to intervene before help comes.

Police officers have also objected to assignments to dangerous locations, particularly where they have felt that some of the danger could be alleviated without hardship to the department or to the public. Thus, they have re-sorted to the New York State courts to challenge manda-tory assignments to locations which are subject to bombing attacks such as the Cuban mission in New York City. This section will focus on some of the legal questions raised by current concerns.

Does federal law protect workers generally from unsafe working conditions?

Most workers, yes. The Occupational Safety and Health Act (OSHA) was passed by Congress in 1970.[39] Among other things, OSHA is directed at improving the safety of the workplace. Under OSHA's authority, the Secretary of Labor promulgated a regulation that permits employees to refuse to perform an assigned task because of a reason-able apprehension of death or serious injury coupled with a reasonable belief that no less drastic alternative is available to the worker other than a refusal to perform the task. This regulation was upheld as a valid exercise of authority delegated to the Secretary of Labor by the Congress in the Supreme Court case of *Whirlpool Corp.* v. *Marshall.* There, two Whirlpool employees had been penalized for refusing to retrieve fallen parts from a wire netting from which a coworker had recently fallen to his death.[40]

Do OSHA and regulations promulgated under it apply to police officers?

No. Section 652 of Title 29 of the United States Code specifically exempts governmental entities—federal, state, and local—from the act's coverage.

Could Congress have included police departments as the types of employers subject to OSHA?

The answer is unclear. The 1976 case of *National League of Cities* v. *Usery* placed a limitation on Congress's normally expansive powers under the commerce clause, where the purported exercise of that power impinges on essential governmental functions of state government.[41] Since there is no question that police protection is an essential function of state and local government, it is possible that Congress, even if it wanted to, could not extend OSHA's coverage to police officers. On the other hand, if such coverage did not seriously disrupt the state police function, it would be permissible.

What avenues are open to police officers who seek to eliminate unnecessarily dangerous conditions from an already dangerous job?

The most realistic prospect for police officers to remove unnecessarily dangerous conditions from the police job is through collective bargaining. While the authors are not aware of a state statute that seeks to extend the type of regulation discussed above to the workplace of police officers, representatives of police officers can certainly champion such issues during contract negotiations.

In addition, a number of New York City officers recently challenged in court the conditions of their duty in bomb-prone locations. In *Miller* v. *McGuire,* ninety-eight police officers began a lawsuit in which they challenged the conditions of their assignment before the Cuban Mission to the United Nations, the U.S. Mission to the United Nations, and the residence of the sister of the Shah of Iran.[42] There had been several bombing attacks at the two U.S. missions in recent months. The officers objected to being forced to stand "immediately in front of" and "on each side of" the Cuban Mission and "immediately in front of" the U.S. Mission. The relief requested was to station officers at a safer distance in patrol cars. In the other case, the officers claimed that twenty-four-hour duty was unnecessary in view of private security forces retained by the Shah's sister. While the deployment practices of the Police Department were challenged on a number of grounds, including violations of the equal-protection clause and of the prohibition against cruel and unusual punishment, it is difficult to conceive of the officers' prevailing on the merits. Without a state statute similar to OSHA, or extension of OSHA to state public-sector employees, the most realistic hope of alleviating what officers see as unnecessarily dangerous working conditions is through collective bargaining.

D. THE OFFICER AND THE COMMUNITY

Relations between police officers and the communities they patrol are often strained. Indeed, reports suggest that such tensions have recently been exacerbated, particularly between police officers and minority populations in large cities. Following the riots in many large cities in the 1960s, police departments made special efforts to equip their officers "with sophisticated techniques for dealing with community revolt." These techniques included training officers to understand minorities better, and hiring substantial numbers of minority-group members to serve on police forces. The positive effect of these efforts may be dissipating in some cities, however, with a consequent rise in police-community tensions. The most extreme recent instance of frayed police-community relations came in the May 1980 race riots in Miami, Florida, which followed the acquittal of four white police officers accused of beating a black businessman to death.[43]

Charges of police brutality have also increased of late. "The Community Relations Service, a part of the Justice Department charged with mediating racial and other disputes, found that in the six-month period ended in April [1980] incidents in which minority groups charged excessive use of police force rose 142 percent over the same period a year ago." [44] Charges of police brutality have often had racial overtones.[45] Indeed the Community Relations Service has reported that, for the six months ended April 1980, there were 336 racial incidents in which minority groups charged excessive force by the police.[46]

Such complaints have, in the past as well as recently, led to calls for greater accountability of police officers to the civilian communities they protect. The mechanisms suggested to achieve such accountability have included civilian review boards, name tags, and internal monitoring procedures.

What is a civilian review board?

A civilian review board can take any of several forms. Detroit's for example, has five civilians appointed by the mayor with consent of the city council. The Detroit board establishes policies, rules, and regulations of the police department; reviews and approves the department's budget; resolves complaints about the department from both civilians and police officers; reviews disciplinary actions; and makes an annual report to the mayor, the city council, and the public. The Detroit board is also balanced racially, consisting of three blacks and two whites.[47]

Civilian oversight may take other forms. The Bar Association of Suffolk County, New York, recently recommended creating a permanent, seven-member panel to investigate future allegations of police brutality. The recommendation, in response to increasing numbers of citizen complaints of brutality, envisages a civilian review board whose duties are much narrower than those of the Detroit board; it would deal only with future charges of brutality.

Another form of civilian review is the grand jury. Upon every shooting by a New York City police officer, a grand jury is empaneled to determine whether the use of force was appropriate or whether criminal sanctions should be sought.[48]

What are the benefits of civilian review boards?

The chairperson of the Detroit Board of Police Commissioners has written glowingly of the benefits of civilian oversight. He has stated that the model utilized in Detroit has brought police-community relations to an all-time high, that crime has continuously declined since the inception of the board, that no police officer has been fatally shot in the last four years, that fatal shootings by police officers have decreased by 39 percent from 1974 to 1978 and by 57 percent for the first six months of 1979, and that the percentage of black and women officers has increased substantially from 1973 to 1979.[49] While the causal relationship between civilian review boards and some of these benefits may be questioned, it seems clear that public accountability of police officers' acts in and of itself is desirable.

Must police officers wear name tags?

Most urban police forces require their members to wear name tags.[50] In New York City, an officer's failure to wear a name tag is an infraction of departmental rules. However, shield numbers are still the official form of identification.

What other mechanisms might be adopted to increase accountability of police officers?

There are many possibilities, but two recent examples prove illustrative. In Kansas City, "police officials began keeping track of officers who were the subject of most complaints of brutality and if cause were found, dismissing them." And in Philadelphia, the police department recently adopted for the first time in the city's history "a written policy governing the use of deadly force by the police." Both mechanisms have reportedly led to significant improvements in police-community relations.[51]

E. POLICE FILES AND THE FREEDOM OF INFORMATION ACT

What is a freedom of information act (FOIA)?

The federal Freedom of Information Act provides that the records of federal agencies shall be made available for review upon the request of "any person," unless the record falls under one of the nine statutory exemptions.[52] The exemptions include classified national-security documents, internal personnel rules and practices; interagency memoranda; personnel, medical, and highly personal files; and certain law-enforcement records. If an exemption applies, the agency that keeps the records may withhold the requested document from disclosure. The purpose of an FOIA is to protect the right of the public to learn about government operations.[53]

Many states have enacted "baby" FOIAs. They tend to be patterned after the federal act and provide that state agency records are available for disclosure to the public, unless exempt.[54]

May police officers use FOIAs to review nonexempt government records?

Yes. FOIAs would not require that the officer (or any other citizen) have a legal interest in seeing the record requested but rather allow "any person" to review any nonexempt agency record.[55]

May FOIAs be used to review agency records concerning police officers?

Yes, unless a statutory exemption applies. The two exemptions most likely to be relevant to police records are the ones protecting privacy and law-enforcement records. The privacy exemption permits withholding "personnel and medical files and similar files [whose] disclosure would constitute a clearly unwarranted invasion of personal privacy." The law-enforcement exemption permits the nondisclosure of:

investigatory records compiled for law-enforcement purposes, but only to the extent that the production of such records would

(A) interfere with enforcement proceedings,
(B) deprive a person of a right to a fair trial or an impartial adjudication,
(C) constitute an unwarranted invasion of personal privacy,
(D) disclose the identity of a confidential source and, in the case of a record compiled by a criminal law-enforcement authority in the course of a criminal investigation, or by an agency conducting a lawful national security intelligence investigation, confidential information furnished only by the confidential source,
(E) disclose investigative techniques and procedures, or
(F) endanger the life or physical safety of law-enforcement personnel.

A third relevant exemption applies to records kept confidential under other laws.

Can the public discover personal information about an officer such as name, salary, educational and employment background, promotional history, and the like?

Probably. Courts have held that

The names and salaries of municipal employees, including disbursements to policemen for off-duty work details, are not the kind of private facts . . . intended to [be] exempt from mandatory disclosure. . . . Even if disclosure of municipal payroll records would bring the right of privacy into play, the paramount right of the public to know what its public servants are paid must prevail.[56]

Date and place of birth, educational background, private and public work experience, and promotion history are also facts subject to disclosure.[57] If the department factually demonstrated that disclosing officers' names and addresses would interfere with law enforcement, however, it probably could withhold these statistics. Moreover, detailed information about an officer's health and family status would probably be protected from disclosure under the FOIA's privacy exemption.

Are records concerning police investigations, "incident reports," and the discharge of weapons subject to disclosure under FOIAs?

Maybe, depending upon the nature and contents of the record sought.

Two federal courts of appeals have held that virtually all FBI investigative records are exempt from FOIA disclosure as records "compiled for law enforcement purposes." [58] The courts reason that the federal law-enforcement exemption is effectively "a description of the type of agency the exemption is aimed at," rather than a requirement as to the use or purpose of the materials requested. Thus, FBI documents that indicate on their face an investigatory character or valid law-enforcement purpose are exempt from disclosure under the federal FOIA.

By comparison, state police records are not subject to a blanket exemption from disclosure under state FOIAs.[59] Rather each such FOIA request must be judged on a case-by-case basis. If the department determines that a record is exempt, the burden rests with it to prove the exemption.[60] Proof must be factual and not hypothetical.

In *Bougas* v. *Chief of Police,* for example, the Massachusetts Supreme Judicial Court upheld the nondisclosure of reports of the Lexington, Massachusetts, police and letters to the police from private citizens regarding an incident resulting in misdemeanor charges against several of the plaintiffs.[61] The court reasoned that the withholding was necessary to avoid prematurely disclosing the state's case prior to trial and disclosing confidential investigative techniques, procedures, and information. The court elaborated that private citizens must be encouraged to communicate with police personnel, and the investigating officer, to record their observations candidly. Disclosure could inhibit such information-gathering.

Compare *Bougas* with *Reinstein* v. *Police Commissioner,* also decided by Massachusetts' highest court.[62] In *Reinstein* the court intimated (but did not rule) that disclosure of information concerning the discharge of firearms by officers "would be of considerable public interest and would offend no legitimate interest on the part of the government or private citizens." [63] Such potentially disclosable information included the amount, time, and place of discharge incidents; the number of incidents when police fired first, and when in response to fire; the number and classification of police disciplinary actions; the number and classification of disciplinary violations; the number of officers actually disciplined; and the substance of recommended changes in discharge regulations. Earlier, the police department had voluntarily disclosed the number and names of persons injured or killed in discharge incidents, presumably after determining that disclosure did not impair law enforcement nor violate the victim's privacy interests.

In sum, the disclosability of state police reports must be decided on a case-by-case basis, by classifying and evaluating the requested information in light of the purposes of the FOIA and its exemptions.

Are arrest and conviction records subject to public disclosure?

A maze of federal and state laws regulate disclosure of the names of arrestees and criminal defendants. For example, state statutes such as those enacted in Massachusetts prevent access to alphabetic court indexes of criminal defendants,[64] records of first offenders under the Controlled Substances Act,[65] and certain probation files and corresponding court records.[66] Where such federal or state statutes prevent the disclosure of criminal records, the FOIA does not apply.[67]

Of course, otherwise confidential criminal records may be subject to disclosure in specific contexts, such as to counsel for a defendant who requests the conviction record of potential government witnesses at trial, or to an inmate requesting to see his or her own probation records.[68] Therefore, persons seeking the disclosure (or nondisclosure) of criminal records should consult federal and state law in their jurisdiction.

Can individual police officers or their unions bring a lawsuit to prevent the disclosure of police records claimed to be exempt under the FOIA?

No. Only the agency that keeps the requested records (typically the police department) can defend against their disclosure.[69] Moreover, even if the department determines that the FOIA exempts the requested documents, the agency retains the discretion to produce the information. In *Chrysler Corp.* v. *Brown*, the Supreme Court unanimously ruled that the FOIA permits but does not compel the withholding of exempt information.[70]

NOTES

1. *See* Foley v. Connelie, 435 U.S. 291, 293 (1978).
2. *E.g.*, Riss v. City of New York, 22 N.Y.2d 579 (1968). *See* Chandler v. District of Columbia, 48 U.S.L.W. 2131 (D.C. Ct. App. Aug. 2, 1979); Grogan v. Kentucky, 577 S.W.2d 4 (Ky. Sup. Ct. 1979); Bruno v. Codd, 64 App. Div. 2d 582, 407 N.Y.S.2d 165 (1st Dep't 1978); Steitz v. City of Beacon, 295 N.Y. 51 (1945). *See generally* note, *Police Liability for Negligent Failure to Prevent Crime*, 94 Harv. L. Rev. 821 (1981).
3. Reiff v. City of Philadelphia, 48 U.S.L.W. 2039 (E.D. Pa. June 25, 1979). *Cf.* Martinez v. California, 48 U.S.L.W. 4076 (U.S. Jan. 15, 1980).

4. 22 N.Y. 2d 579 (1968).

5. Id. at 584 (Keating, J., dissenting).

6. Id. at 581 (majority opinion).

7. Id. at 581–82.

8. Id. at 584–94.

9. Reiff v. City of Philadelphia, 48 U.S.L.W. 2039 (E.D. Pa. June 25, 1979) (§1983).

10. Bruno v. Codd, 64 App. Div. 2d 582, 407 N.Y.S. 2d 165 (1st Dep't 1978).

11. Chandler v. District of Columbia, 48 U.S.L.W. 2131 (D.C. Ct. App. Aug. 2, 1979).

12. See 47 U.S.L.W. 2085 (Aug. 8, 1978).

13. See Thompson v. County of Alameda, 49 U.S.L.W. 2074 (Cal. Sup. Ct. July 14, 1980); Schuster v. City of New York, 5 N.Y. 2d 75, 82 (1958). Cf. Lipari v. Sears Roebuck, 49 U.S.L.W. 2121 (D. Neb. July 17, 1980); Tarasoff v. Regents of the University of California, 17 Cal. 3d 425, 551 P.2d 334, 131 Cal. Rptr. 14 (1976); McIntosh v. Milano, 48 U.S.L.W. 2039 (N.J. Super. Ct. June 12, 1979); Restatement (Second) of Torts §315.

14. Washington Post, Dec. 25, 1980, at A1, col. 1 (D.C. Court of Appeals rules that victim can sue police for inaction where police had assured victim that assistance would be forthcoming and victim relied on the promised assistance); Schuster v. City of New York, 5 N.Y.2d 75, 82–83, 86–89 (1958) (McNally, J., concurring). See Moch Co. v. Rensselaer Water Co., 247 N.Y. 160, 167–68 (1928).

15. 5 N.Y.2d 75 (1958) (Van Voorhis, J.).

16. Id. at 87–88 (McNally, J., concurring).

17. Id. at 80–81 (Van Voorhis, J.).

18. Id. at 82. Accord, id. at 86–88 (McNally, J., concurring) ("The assumption by the [police] of the partial protection of [the citizen] under the circumstances of this case carried with it the obligation not to terminate such protection if in the exercise of reasonable care . . . [such termination] either enlarged or prolonged the risk of bodily harm" to the citizen).

19. C.A. No. 79–6 (D.C. Ct. App. Dec. 24, 1980), discussed in National L.J. at 3, 6 (Jan. 19, 1981) and in Wash. Post, Dec. 25, 1980, at A1, col. 1.

20. Also, see Morgan v. County of Yuba, 230 Cal. App.2d 938, Silverman v. City of Fort Wayne, 357 N.E. 20 285

(Ind. App. 1976); Bloom v. City of New York, 357 N.Y.S. 2d 981; Florence v. Goldberg, 404 N.Y.S.2d 583 (1978).

21. McCrink v. City of New York, 296 N.Y. 99 (1945).

22. 48 U.S.L.W. 4076 (U.S. Jan. 15, 1980).

23. *Id.* at 4078 (footnotes omitted).

24. *Id.* at 4077.

25. 5 N.Y.2d 75 (1958).

26. Riss v. City of New York, 22 N.Y.2d 579 (1968). *See* Kenny v. SEPTA, 581 F.2d 351 (3d Cir), *cert. denied,* 439 U.S. 1073 (1978).

27. RESTATEMENT (SECOND) OF TORTS §344 (1965).

28. 581 F.2d 351 (3d Cir.), *cert. denied,* 439 U.S. 1073 (1978).

29. Hubbard v. Buelt, 49 U.S.L.W. 2439 (Cal. Dec. 15, 1980) ("fireman's rule" bars tort suits by police officers based on citizen's negligence in creating situation requiring police action).

30. *See generally* W. PROSSER, LAW OF TORTS §9, at 34–37 (4th ed. 1971).

31. *Id.* §§119–20, at 834–56.

32. *Id.* §121, at 856.

33. *Id.* (footnote omitted).

34. *Id.*

35. *Id.* at 857 (footnote omitted).

36. N.Y. Times, Jan. 30, 1980, at 1, col. 4; Mar. 9, 1980, at E7, col. 1.

37. *See* Miller v. McGuire, No. 05358/80, *petition filed,* March 25, 1980 (Sup. Ct., New York County).

38. *See* note 36 *supra.*

39. 29 U.S.C. §§651–78.

40. 48 U.S.L.W. 4189 (U.S. Feb. 26, 1980).

41. 426 U.S. 833 (1976).

42. *See* Miller v. McGuire, No. 05358/80, *petition filed,* March 25, 1980 (Sup. Ct., New York County).

43. N.Y. Times, May 15, 1980, at 16, col. 1.

44. *Id.*

45. N.Y. Times, Jan. 30, 1980, at B4, col. 4.

46. N.Y. Times, May 15, 1980, at 16, col. 1.

47. N.Y. Times, Feb. 23, 1980 (letter to editor).

48. Interview with Kenneth Conboy, Deputy Commissioner, New York City Police Department (April 4, 1980).

49. *See* note 47 *supra.*

50. *See* note 48 *supra;* Slocum v. Fire and Police Commission of East Peoria, 8 Ill. App. 3d 465, 290 N.E.2d 28 (1972).

51. N.Y. Times, May 15, 1980, at 16, col. 1.

52. 5 U.S.C. §552 (1976).

53. *See* Department of Air Force v. Rose, 425 U.S. 352 (1976); Hastings & Sons Publ. Co. v. City Treasurer of Lynn, 1978 Mass. Adv. Sh. 920, 375 N.E.2d 299 (Apr. 18, 1978).

54. *E.g.*, MASS. GEN. LAWS ANN. ch. 66, §10 (West 1980 Supp.).

55. *See* Bougas v. Chief of Police, 371 Mass. 59 (1976); Cunningham v. Health Officer, 1979 Mass. App. Ct. Adv. Sh. 178, 179 (Feb. 14, 1979). *See also* Doyle v. Dept. of Justice, 49 U.S.L.W. 2085 (D.D.C. July 22, 1980).

56. Hastings & Sons Publ. Co. v. City Treasurer of Lynn, 1978 Mass. Adv. Sh. at 927–29, 375 N.E.2d at 304. *See* Attorney General v. Collector of Lynn, 1979 Mass. Adv. Sh. 191, 198 (Jan. 26, 1979).

57. Simpson v. Vance, 49 U.S.L.W. 2246 (D.C. Cir. Sept. 25, 1980).

58. *See* Kuehnert v. FBI, 48 U.S.L.W. 2751 (8th Cir. Apr. 29, 1980), *interpreting* 5 U.S.C. §555(b) (7) (1976); Irons v. Bell, 594 F.2d 468 (1st Cir. 1979). *Cf.* Murphy v. FBI, 48 U.S.L.W. 2813 (D.D.C. May 28, 1980) (FBI ABSCAM tapes may be withheld from disclosure under law-enforcement exemption (A)). *See also* Sims v. CIA, 49 U.S.L.W. 2278 (D.C. Cir. Sept. 29, 1980); Simpson v. Vance, 49 U.S.L.W. 2246 (D.C. Cir. Sept. 25, 1980).

59. Bougas v. Chief of Police, 371 Mass. 59 (1976), *Accord*, Reinstein v. Police Commissioner, 1979 Mass. Adv. Sh. 1509 (June 20, 1979).

60. *E.g.*, MASS. GEN. LAWS ANN. ch. 66, §10 (West Supp. 1980). *Accord*, Attorney General v. School Committee of Northampton, 1978 Mass. Adv. Sh. 1108, 1115, 375 N.E.2d 1188, 1191 (Apr. 27, 1978); Bougas v. Chief of Police, 371 Mass. at 71.

61. 371 Mass. 59 (1979).

62. 1979 Mass. Adv. Sh. 1509 (June 20, 1979).

63. *Id.* at 1516–17.

64. MASS. GEN. LAWS ANN. ch. 6, §172 (West Supp. 1979) (the Criminal Offender Record Information Act).

65. MASS. GEN. LAWS ANN. ch. 94C, §34 (West Supp. 1979).

66. MASS. GEN. LAWS ANN. ch. 276, §§100A, 100B, 100C (West Supp. 1979). *See also* Carson v. Dep't of Justice, 49 U.S.L.W. 2211 (D.C.Cir. Aug. 27, 1980).

67. *E.g.*, 5 U.S.C. §552(b)(3) (1976).
68. *E.g.*, Crooker v. Foley, 8 Mass. Lawyers Weekly 665, Lawyers Weekly No. J38 (Mass. Super. Ct. 1980) (FOIA "privacy" exemption does not preclude person from viewing records pertaining to that individual).
69. *See* Chrysler Corp. v. Brown, 441 U.S. 281, 290–94 (1979); GTE Sylvania, Inc. v. Consumers Union of the United States, Inc., 48 U.S.L.W. 4293, 4293 n. 2 (U.S. Mar. 19, 1980).
70. 441 U.S. 281 (1979).

Index